Answering the ...**Guy** Questions

Leslie Ludy

HARVEST HOUSE PUBLISHERS

EUGENE, OREGON

Cover by Abris, Veneta, Oregon

Leslie Ludy: Published in association with Loyal Arts Literary Agency, LoyalArts.com.

ANSWERING THE GUY QUESTIONS
Copyright © 2009 by Winston and Brooks, Inc.
Published by Harvest House Publishers
Eugene, Oregon 97402
www.harvesthousepublishers.com

Library of Congress Cataloging-in-Publication Data
Ludy, Leslie.
Answering the guy questions / Leslie Ludy.
    p. cm.
ISBN 978-0-7369-2287-6 (pbk.)
1. Young women—Religious life. 2. Man-woman relationships—Religious aspects—Christianity. I. Title.
BV4551.3.L825 2009
248.8'43—dc22

                                                                            2008036844

Contents

A Christ-Consumed Heart

putting first things first

The set-apart women I admire most all had one very important thing in common—they were passionately, ardently, fervently in love with Jesus Christ. They put Jesus Christ above pleasures, riches, comforts, friends, family, and worldly applause. And they put Jesus Christ far above guys.

Amy Carmichael sacrificed her right to be married and, instead, chose to spend her life rescuing a thousand children from being sold into temple prostitution in India. Her romance with Jesus Christ far exceeded the most beautiful fairy tale ever written.

Sabina Wurmbrand sacrificed her right to live "happily ever after" with the love of her life, Richard, when she was forced to make a choice between saving her husband and standing up for her first love, Jesus Christ. By choosing Jesus, she inspired her husband to stand against those who were blaspheming Christ's name, and as a result, she and Richard were separated for ten long years.

Gladys Aylward spent all of her youth and beauty in a war-torn Chinese village. Rather than pining after men and pursuing marriage, family, and the comforts of this world, Gladys chose a life of service for the kingdom of God. As a result, a hundred violent prisoners were subdued into quiet obedience, two hundred orphans were saved, and thousands were pulled out of darkness and into God's marvelous light.

Catherine Booth laid down her right to a comfortable marriage and family life. Not only did her husband pour out his life for the destitute and dying, but Catherine joined him, serving right by his side. She chose all-night prayer gatherings, long days trudging through slums, and attacks from the modern church over a stable existence in a cute home with a white picket fence.

When I study these women's lives, I am astounded and inspired by their level of commitment to Jesus Christ. They didn't just *say* He was their first love—they lived it. Though they gave up their rights to be married and their dreams of living the "happily ever after" lifestyle, nothing was more important than serving Christ and protecting the honor of their Lord and King.

So it must be with us.

Even though this is a book about guys, I want to emphasize that Jesus Christ, not guys, must always remain the center of our existence. When we have a Christ-consumed heart, guys no longer dominate our thoughts, our actions, and our decisions. Rather, the Lover of our soul captivates us so completely that every guy we meet clearly sees that Jesus is, and always will be, the number one Prince of our heart. These lyrics from a song by According to John capture this idea beautifully:

She's in Love

What a beautiful smile; A radiant girl
Fell in love first time I saw her; She stays on my mind
I'd give anything; To know everything about her

There's light in her eyes; And I know it's all for Him
She carries on and on; Like He was her best friend

Chorus:
  She's in love; It's not hard to see
  But I would like to believe it was with me
  Someone got a hold of her heart
  And He won't let go
  And I know; She's in love

She looks to the sky; When she talks about Him
She believes He hung the moon; Said He had to go away
She waits for His return; Says He's coming for her soon

How can this be fair?
This guy can walk on water
Don't guess I've got a prayer
He's written love letters to reach her

She worships the ground He walks on
She just smiles when she says His name
It's a match made in heaven
I can't compete with the King of Kings[1]

—ACCORDING TO JOHN

Until a guy can truly say *that* about your life, you aren't ready for an earthly "Prince Charming." Until Jesus Christ is the obsession of your heart, you'll always be looking to mere men to meet needs only He can fill.

So even though this book is filled with practical advice about relating to guys, let me warn you not to become consumed with the subject of the opposite sex. When you become consumed with Jesus Christ, dealing with guys becomes far less confusing!

I can honestly say that if you live out the lyrics of that song, all of the romantic desires of your heart will be fulfilled—whether you end up with an earthly Prince Charming or not. Making Jesus Christ your first love is the foundation for everything else in life, including guys. If you feel uncertain about His position in your life, read *Authentic Beauty* and *Set-Apart Femininity*, in which I explore intimacy with Christ in a very practical and in-depth way.

This book is meant to be a practical tool in your hands—a fleshing out of what set-apart femininity looks like in relationship to masculinity. Through the years, countless young women have come to me with questions about guys. And to the best of my ability, I've attempted to answer the most common ones and place them within the pages of this book. I like to write my books as if I am sitting across from you, my reader, in a cozy coffee shop, simply sharing my heart. I hope you'll feel that way as you read through the following chapters filled with advice and encouragement. Think of me as a big sister who has gone before you and wants to share everything she's learned on the subject of guys.

You'll notice that I refer to my love story with my husband, Eric, quite a few times. I hope you won't feel that I'm suggesting that the specific details of my love story need to be imitated.

Rather, it's my desire to give you a real-life example of what these biblical principles look like lived out.

This book is very straightforward, keeping with the lovingly blunt personality God blessed me with! My message sets a high standard for interaction with the opposite sex, and I don't apologize for it because I believe it's the standard of Christ. And I also believe that if you are willing to take this message to heart, you'll experience an amazing, astounding, heaven-on-earth blessing just like I did. My prayer is that through these pages you'll be inspired, encouraged, and equipped to approach this area of your life with Christ-built confidence rather than culture-induced confusion!

Please know that I am cheering you on in your set-apart journey. I would love for you to visit my website, www.setapartgirl.com, where there are many additional resources, such as audio sessions and articles, to encourage and equip you along the way.

If you've picked up this book, I don't believe it's a coincidence. I know God has an incredible purpose for you and can use this message in your life. His plans for you are more beautiful than you could hope or imagine, and I pray that this book will be an instrumental part of your walk with Him.

Set-apart femininity can change the world. May this book inspire you to fully realize this reality.

Cheering you on!

Leslie

CHAPTER ONE

Counterfeit Manhood

the way modern guys are versus
the way God wants them to be

In seventh grade, boys were my nemesis.

Boys were loud and obnoxious, insensitive and crude. At the age of twelve, I was painfully awkward, shy and insecure—and this unfortunate combination smacked a bright red "easy target" sign in the middle my forehead. Every morning on the bus ride to school, I was mercilessly tormented by a gangly, puberty-stricken clamor of testosterone. Max Johnson, the ringleader, seemed to think it was his personal mission in life to demonstrate his masculine superiority over all womankind by using me as a verbal punching bag in front of his friends. His specific put-downs were a bit too profane for me to include in this book, but suffice it to say that, using many creative and perverted metaphors, Max deemed me unfeminine, unsexy, and wholly undesirable to the male species.

I hated seventh-grade boys. They made my life miserable. Nearly all of them had this annoyingly arrogant, strut-on-the-beach-like-Tom-Cruise-in-*Top-Gun* attitude, conveniently overlooking the fact that they could barely bench-press 45 pounds, didn't have enough facial hair to warrant owning a razor, and had to ride a big yellow bus to school because they weren't old enough to drive. Taking their cues from older brothers and pop-culture role models, they treated every girl like a piece of meat to either lustfully consume or carelessly discard—depending on the level of her sex appeal. I ranked dismally low on that sexiness scale. Like an overcooked steak, I was chewed up and spit out by Max and his gang of Hollywood heartthrob wannabes.

But it wasn't just their ridiculous display of male ego that made me despise them. It was the paralyzing fear that when it came to guys, this was all I could ever expect.

Like every other American female, I'd grown up with the fairy tales. I knew what kind of man I wanted to end up with someday. I wanted a gentleman—someone who would stand up for me, cherish me, find me beautiful, and have eyes for no other woman but me. I wanted a man who wasn't just interested in my physical appearance, but someone who took delight in exploring the deepest caverns of my heart and soul. I wanted a true hero—a guy who didn't just talk a big talk, but someone marked by masculine nobility and honor. I wanted a guy who was selfless—a guy who would give his life to protect those weaker than himself. I wanted a gallant knight.

But by the age of twelve, I was starting to awaken to the fact that I wasn't living in a fairy tale. On the contrary, I seemed to be living in a warped, counter-fairy-tale reality, where the most "noble" act a man seemed capable of was putting the toilet seat down after using it, and the most "faithful" of men were those who chose to live out their illicit fantasies via Internet porn rather than have an actual affair. The majority of my friends' parents were divorced, and most of the married men I observed had so completely tuned out their wives that they might as well have been bachelors.

Happily, my own parents had a beautiful marriage, and my dad was both noble and sensitive. He was (and is) a wonderful husband and father and had none of the crude or debased tendencies so common among modern males. Witnessing his version of masculinity allowed me to hold on to the tiny shred of hope that maybe it was actually possible to end up with a heroic prince someday. But the older I grew, the less hopeful I became.

After countless bus rides filled with the taunting jeers and disgusting bathroom humor of Max Johnson and his cohorts, I was beginning to think that I would never be so fortunate as to find a guy whose personality was even one step beyond the dismal standards of Beavis and Butt-head. And judging by most of the older brothers and dads I observed, men didn't seem to change much between seventh grade and full-grown adulthood. My friend Staci's older brother—a cocky basketball player with spiked hair and a nose ring—spent all of his spare time concocting poems and short stories detailing various sexual acts and then circulating these literary masterpieces around his high school until they were legendary. My neighbor Tyler started getting condoms and sex advice from his dad at the age of 13. "Always keep a couple of them in your wallet," Tyler's dad instructed him, "and when you get the chance to score with a hot girl, don't wimp out! If you haven't had sex with at least ten different girls by the time you graduate from high school, I'll be ashamed to call you my son."

By the time I reached high school I had completely given up on the idea of finding a Prince Charming. Most guys I knew hung posters of bikini-clad supermodels on their bedroom walls and carried *Playboy* magazines to school in their backpacks. They implied that any high school girls they dated were merely stand-ins until they finally had the chance to hook up with their *real* fantasy—a Victoria's Secret or *Playboy* centerfold model (conveniently overlooking the fact that they could never snag that kind of woman in the first place). Like countless other girls, I became jaded by the sex-obsessed minds of modern guys. I was plagued by insecurity, knowing that no matter how physically attractive I became, I could never measure up to the culture's impossible standards for feminine sex appeal, and thus, I could never really capture the heart of a modern guy.

The extra discouraging wrinkle to the whole saga was that Christian guys didn't seem much different than all the other warped, perverted men of modern times. In fact, my youth pastor, Kevin Richards, greeted me (and several other girls) each week as we entered the youth room with a sly smile and the question, "So, who's your boyfriend this week?" Kevin didn't act much different from the rest of the guys in the room—he flirted with the attractive girls and ignored all the others. From my perspective, it seemed that even my Christian male leader seemed to see girls the way all the other guys did—merely there for the pleasure and enjoyment of men. If we weren't hopping from boyfriend to boyfriend, then Kevin implied that we were abnormal. And if we weren't with a guy, we seemed to have very little purpose or value in his eyes.

In the hallways at my high school, I constantly overheard guys lustfully describe girls' bodies (and the sexual acts they desired to do with them) in pornographic detail. The one time I actually got up the nerve to confront a guy about his perverted attitude toward girls, he told me, "This is just the way guys are—get over it."

Though I was discouraged and disgusted by the state of modern masculinity, I was desperately afraid of being unappealing to the opposite sex. Like most other girls my age, I reasoned that being treated like a sex object was better than being disregarded by guys and spending the rest of my life alone. So I began catering to the masculine perversion all around me by dressing seductively to gain male approval, laughing carelessly when guys touched or grabbed me sexually in the school halls, and giving away my heart, emotions, and almost all of my physical purity to one casual, meaningless fling after another. Like most other girls my age, giving in to the dismal standard of modern masculinity left me heartbroken, wounded, and plagued with debilitating insecurity. My feminine heart still longed for Prince Charming, but reality convinced me that my desire for a noble knight was an immature, idiotic dream that could never come true and that I was destined to end up with a self-focused, egotistical man who would always be lusting after other women, even after he had pledged his heart to me.

Popular urban legend states that men think about sex approximately every seven seconds. Though there is no way to actually prove such a statement, simply being around modern guys seems to validate that rumor as scientific fact. It's a catch-22, if you think about it. The culture sends a clear message to boys, from the time they are old enough to even notice the opposite sex, that they are not normal unless they are fixated on the female body. It becomes a self-fulfilling prophecy—boys want to be seen as masculine, so they eagerly step into the role that society creates for them, becoming sex-obsessed cavemen incapable of seeing women as anything more than pieces of meat to be lustfully devoured. The result is the perverted, sex-addicted version of manhood we see all around us. And in case we ever doubt the severity of the problem, all we must do is take a look at these startling facts:

- Nearly 28 million guys visit at least one Internet porn site every month.[1]
- The largest group of viewers of Internet porn is children between the ages of 12 and 17.[2]
- The Internet porn industry generates 12 billion dollars in annual revenue—more than the combined annual revenue of ABC, CBS, and NBC.[3]

Though the Christian men of our culture are supposed to be the ones who will rise above the debased mediocrity around them, they are just as ensnared by the same warped perspective and sinful sexual vices as the rest of their male counterparts. In fact, the church is literally inundated with pastors, leaders, and Christ-professing men who are enslaved to Internet porn, premarital sex, adulterous affairs, and even homosexuality. According to a 2001 leadership survey of clergy who had Internet access, 51 percent said Internet pornography is a possible temptation, and 37 percent said it is a current struggle—and these were just the ones who were actually being honest when polled.[4]

Even more disturbing is the defeated attitude that we as Christians have taken toward this issue. Not long ago I sat in a pastor's office as he criticized a wife for being offended at her husband's pornography addiction. "He's not a pervert or a sex addict," the pastor said. "He's just a normal, red-blooded male. Every guy deals with this, and it's time we stop making men feel ashamed about it."

While I understand the reasoning behind such an attitude, I also believe it is extremely dangerous. Men with sexual addictions should not be mercilessly condemned by the church—as in, "you are a hopeless, disgusting pervert, and God wants nothing to do with you." However, we have swung in the opposite direction, embracing and accepting men's sex-obsessed state without expecting them to be set free by the transforming grace of God.

I can't even count the number of young women who have written over the past few years, telling me about sexual compromise within their church. Some of them have been sexually assaulted by their youth pastors. Others have engaged in secret affairs with pastors or worship leaders. Still others were sexually abused by their fathers—some of whom were elders, deacons, or leaders in the church.

A young man who just graduated from a Christian college told me, "The problem of sexual perversion is beyond rampant—even in the church. Having just come out of a Christian college, I can tell you categorically that there's not a guy I met who wasn't either struggling with lust or completely given over to it. Many even seemed to take some pride in the fact."

Why are Christian men more defeated by sexual sin than ever before? I believe that it's largely because Christian men are inundated with voices that excuse slothful, sinful mediocrity rather than call them to the righteous standard of Christ. The biblical principle of consecrating our bodies as the temple of the Most High God is conveniently ignored, while the worldly prescription "just do what feels good" reigns supreme.

In a popular Christian book for men, the author writes about his *current* struggle with a defeated marriage and temptation toward sin:

> As I write this chapter, [my wife] and I have just returned from a friend's wedding. It was one of the best nuptials either of us have ever been to...the groom was young and strong and valiant, the bride was seductively beautiful. Which is what made it so excruciating for me...[my wife] and I were in a difficult place over the weekend. Satan saw his opportunity and turned it into a bonfire without even one word between us. By the time we got to the reception, I didn't want to dance with her. I didn't even want to be in the same room. All the hurt and disappointment of the years— hers and mine—seemed to be the only thing that was ever true about our marriage. [I thought] "I'm so tired of battling for our marriage. How I wish we could start over. It wouldn't be that hard, you know. Look at all these beautiful women." On and on it came, like a wave overwhelming the shore. Sitting at the table with a group of our friends, I felt I was going to suffocate; I had to get out of there, get some fresh air. Truth be told, when I left the reception I had no intention of going back. Either I'd wind up in a bar somewhere or back in our room watching T.V. Thankfully I found a small library off the reception hall—I grabbed a book but could not read, I tried to pray but I did not want to. Finally some words began to arise from my heart, "Jesus, come and rescue my heart before I do something stupid."[5]

In that same book, the author described another situation in which he became so irritated with his wife—she suggested a different route than the one they had been driving—that he literally would have divorced her on the spot if he'd had the opportunity.

What a far cry from the fairy tale we all dream about! This is the reality of most marriages, even Christian ones. As women, we assume that it's normal to be married to a man who, in the space of one weekend, can get so disgruntled with his marriage that he describes another man's wife as "seductively beautiful," refuses to even be in the same room with his wife after an argument, and notices every other beautiful woman in the room, wishing he could "start over" with one of them. Most modern Christians treat a scenario like this as perfectly acceptable, which is why nobody made a fuss over this disturbing section of that book. But as I read about such blatant masculine defeat, I can't help but think, *if that is the best we can expect from a Christian marriage, why would we want to get married at all? If that is the standard by which Christian husbands (and even well-known leaders) think and act toward their wives, it's no wonder Christian marriages are crumbling left and right and sexual sin wreaks havoc in countless Christ-professing lives.*

This author is merely attempting to be honest with his struggles—and I commend him for being real rather than hypocritical. However, as a Christian leader whom thousands of men esteem, his example of mediocrity is just one more excuse for men to yield to the voice of their sinful, selfish flesh (that is *do what feels good*) rather than the Spirit of God. Yes, the author escaped "doing something stupid" in regard to his marriage—but not triumphantly. He *yielded* to the voice of his sinful selfish nature from the moment that wedding began. He gave in to lust, self-pity, and selfishness. Rather than crying out to God for power to be victorious over sin, he left the reception hall fully intending to satisfy the cravings of his flesh—by going to a bar or a hotel room to watch TV. And even after sharing this story, he blamed the entire struggle on lies from the enemy instead of willfully yielding to sin on his part.

Christianity has accepted the attitude that "guys are just built this way; they can't help it, so let's not make them feel bad." Thus, men are being carried away like helpless victims to selfishness, lust, and sexual addiction. Not long after that particular men's book was released, the pastor of one of the largest churches in our area confessed to cheating on his wife. He admitted that the pressures of ministry had taken their toll on his marriage and family, and in order to "escape and unwind," he went on a vacation (by himself, leaving his wife and kids at home). How did he spend his much-needed getaway? Not in prayer. Not in focused pursuit of God. Rather, he hung out in bars—and in his hotel room watching TV. It was almost like he was mimicking the book's scenario exactly. Only in his case, he *did* end up "doing something stupid" and sleeping with another woman. Ironically, when he confessed his sin to his church body, they gave him a standing ovation. They were far more impressed with the fact that he was "real" enough to admit his struggle than they were concerned that their Christ-professing leader was defeated by sin and selfishness.

Yet another church in our area—one of the largest in the nation—recently announced that their pastor had fallen into a life-style of deceit and sexual sin. And again, it was when he "escaped" from his wife and children and went off for a self-indulgent get-away to a big city hotel that he caved to one of the many sexual temptations that presented itself in that environment.

This may be the reality of modern Christian men, *but it is not God's intention for masculinity.* Here is just a sampling of what Scripture says about guys and sexual purity:

> You have heard that it was said to those of old, "You shall not commit adultery." But I say to you that whoever looks at a woman to lust for her has already committed adultery with her in her heart. If your right eye causes you to sin, pluck it

out and cast it from you; for it is more profitable for you that one of your members perish, than for your whole body to be cast into hell. And if your right hand causes you to sin, cut it off and cast it from you; for it is more profitable for you that one of your members perish, than for your whole body to be cast into hell (Matthew 5:27-30).

~~~

I have made a covenant with my eyes; why then should I look upon a young woman? If my heart has been enticed by a woman, or if I have lurked at my neighbor's door...that would be wickedness; yes, it would be iniquity deserving of judgment. For that would be a fire that consumes to destruction, and would root out all my increase (Job 31:1,9,11-12).

So how are we, as women, supposed to respond to the vast cavern between the righteous standard of Christ and the disturbing reality of modern masculinity? Thus far, we haven't been given the right answer. I have read several books and magazine articles for Christian women that seek to help us live with guys' lust problems in an understanding, no-nagging, noncritical way. "We as women can't possibly understand a man's intense sex-drive," they exhort us, "and it's time we stop making them feel like criminals for just doing what comes naturally to them."

Criticism, nagging, or heaping guilt upon men, to be sure, will not help a man battling sex addictions and perversion. But neither will shrugging our shoulders and saying, "guys will be guys."

What modern masculinity needs is a serious shot of the *saving, redeeming, transforming, delivering power of Jesus Christ.*

And as women, it's time we realize that we play a significant role in seeing that come about. If you have ever been discouraged, disgusted, depressed, or even defeated by the state of modern masculinity, this book can infuse you with vision, hope, and a practical means of doing something about it.

The problems of modern manhood are not too big for God. He has a huge vision for His men—the very standard of Jesus Christ. And if you are willing, you can be a part of one of the most amazing, God-inspired reformations in history—a radical return of manhood as God intended it to be, in all of its glory, strength, nobility, and honor.

Imposter Manhood Exposed

Our culture has reduced sex to nothing more than a self-gratifying, animalistic impulse rather than a beautiful expression of life-long, fairy-tale love.

When it comes to sex, we seem to be presented with only two options: Succumb to the twisted, selfish, perverted kind of sex blatantly displayed by the media, seeing it as a sinful, shameful, and guilt-ridden area of our lives, or grit our teeth and put up with the "purity route," forcing ourselves to forgo the pleasures of premarital sex only to end up with a dismal, lifeless, not-tonight-honey-I-have-a-headache version of sex in marriage. But there is a secret third option that most of us overlook—it's called God's perfect design for sex. When we encounter God's true design for sex, we experience the most sacred, perfect, beautiful act of nobility and love—far beyond a fairy tale. The culture has warped sex into a cheap imposter of the glorious "real thing" created by the Author of love and romance. And when we exchange the counterfeit for the original, contrary to popular belief, we don't end up with a stuffy, no-fun, mediocre version of sex. *We end up with the fulfillment of all our romantic dreams.* God's version of sex is light years beyond the debased version we see around us today.

But most of us don't realize that there is anything better, so we don't pursue it. We settle for an imposter version and wonder why we feel so unhappy, unsatisfied, and unfulfilled.

Counterfeit masculinity is a lot like counterfeit sex. Men are presented with several dismal options for masculinity, all of which are cheap knockoffs of what God intended. But God's original design for masculinity is a glorious, heroic, triumphant, valiant display of world-altering manhood. The problem is that, just like sex, we don't realize that there is anything better, so we don't pursue it. It's time to uproot counterfeit masculinity and expose it as the sham it really is.

Metro Males

You may have noticed in recent years that a large segment of the modern male population has begun swinging toward the more sensitive, groomed, and socially polished pattern of the metro male. Sweat, dirt, and grunts are being exchanged for sleek hairstyles, facials, and tanning salons. But before you get too excited

Most modern guys don't even believe that they can be anything other than animalistic and given over to their lusts. They use their God-given grit and tenacity to fight for everything but what they were intended to defend and protect (God's truth and the oppressed). I, for one, am ready to see that pattern shift! I desire to marry a man who exhibits the life of Christ in his relationships, ministry, free time—someone who is Christ-like even when he is alone, someone who continues to pursue a deeper relationship with God at all times. I desire to marry a man who doesn't take his role as the spiritual leader and head of our family lightly. My heart longs for a man who has used his single years to learn to protect the women in his life (his sisters, friends, etc.) and to fight for truth.

—COURTNEY, 23

over their exfoliated skin and manicured fingernails, let's take a closer look at the roots of metro masculinity.

What is metro manhood? After countless years of enduring loud, smelly, obnoxious, insensitive, rude, unromantic, burpin', scratchin' specimens of manhood, the women of our culture finally decided enough was enough. Recruiting the help of the gay community and the fashion industry, women began to put pressure on guys to clean up their act, become more refined, and get in touch with their feminine side. The fashion and beauty industry was only too happy to pounce on the opportunity—pushing products to men that include lotions, tanning creams, male manicures, and hair dyes and highlights. Ultrahip men now wear women's pants and pointy shoes with shameless force. Magazines, billboards, the media, and celebrities have united with the mantra, "Girly men are sexy men!" The gay community began lending a helping hand, offering makeover shows like *Queer Eye for the Straight Guy* and other such efforts to proclaim that gay men are in touch with their feminine side and, therefore, understand what makes a man truly appealing to a woman.

The media, the fashion industry, the gay community, and most of womankind have joined forces to cleanse the dirt and grit from masculinity and transform men from frogs into princes. But unfortunately, metro men are becoming a bit more like *heroines* than heroes in this bizarre fairy-tale-gone-awry. One modern writer says,

> Remember the big to-do about whether or not real men ate quiche? Well now not only are they eating quiche, they're wearing salmon colored dress shirts; getting manicures and pedicures; having their hair highlighted; frequenting tanning salons; and are enjoying overall makeovers.[6]

A female journalist for *The Washington Post* writes,

> At dinner the other night, my date listed the calorie count of the main entrees, raising an eyebrow at my chicken Alfredo selection after he had ordered a salad. I saw him check his reflection in the silver water pitcher three times. During dessert, he looked deeply into my eyes and told me he thought what we have together is very special. It was our third date. It was then that I realized why my dating life has been as mysterious as the Bermuda Triangle since I arrived in Washington. This city, unlike any other place I've lived, is a haven for the metrosexual.[7]

And then there is the online Urban Dictionary, in which a straightforward contributor defines metrosexual as:

> A straight homie that acts like a gay dude for some unknown reason.[8]

The bottom line—metro males are guys who act a bit more like women than men. While the popular belief is that women applaud this soft-spoken, sensitive, socially groomed rendition of manhood, in reality the metro version of masculinity falls far short of what women really desire. When you take the "manly stuff" out of masculinity, as my friend Jeremy says, you are left with "weak men and unprotected women." Every young girl (until she is brainwashed by our culture's feminist agenda) dreams of a heroic knight who will slay the evil dragon on her behalf and carry her away to his castle. Metro men are too concerned about maintaining the cleanliness of their designer jeans and the perfect position of their spiked hair to actually get their hands dirty protecting a woman.

Don't get me wrong, I am not against men smelling sweeter, dressing nicer, and exhibiting better table manners. In fact, my husband, Eric, has written for years about "warrior-poet" man-hood—contending that guys are meant to showcase the strength *and* sensitivity of Jesus Christ. Christ-built manhood is not just sweat, blood, and battle cries. It's also compassion, tenderness, nobility, and dignity. But metro manhood is a twisted counterfeit of the "poet" side of masculinity. For one thing, metro manhood emphasizes only a man's soft side, completely disregarding the *strength* and *grit* that men were created to exude. And secondly, it looks to the fashion industry and gay community—rather than the example of Christ—to define the kind of sensitivity, nobility, and dignity God created men to display. The result is a watered-down, mediocre version of masculinity that gives guys an excuse to be self-indulgent, lazy, wimpy, and shockingly feminine.

Many Christian guys I know even wear women's pants, lip gloss, and eyeliner in an attempt to vibe with the metro crowd. I am personally not sure how women can possibly find this attractive, but my opinion doesn't seem to hold much weight against the doctrine of the Fab Five.

Christian metros have allowed the culture to define their masculinity. They have conveniently morphed Scripture to be a bit more accommodating to modern times. They overlook the stunning displays of God-infused manly strength presented all

I am so disheartened by the interaction between husbands and wives and daughters and fathers. I want to see men step up and be strong Christlike men, but I realize that we as women have a lot to do with that. Unless women learn to honor men and hold them to a higher standard, we will never see men rise up to be masculine in the way God intended and created masculinity to be.

—ASHLEY, 24

throughout Scripture: David killed a lion and a bear with his bare hands, Joshobeam single-handedly defeated 800 Philistines, Samson annihilated entire armies with the jawbone of a donkey, Josiah ruthlessly ground to dust all the idols of false gods, and Elijah called down fire from heaven and slayed 350 false prophets, causing the Brook Kishon to overflow with their blood. (Somehow I can't imagine these mighty men of God doing such valiant exploits in women's pants and lip gloss.) And then there is the example of Christ. Yes, He displayed incredible tenderness, humility, and compassion—healing the sick, embracing children, and referring to Himself as the Good Shepherd. But He also exuded superhuman strength and power—calming winds and waves, walking on water, driving out the temple money changers with a whip, walking through the midst of an angry mob that was trying to cast Him off a cliff, and conquering sin and death by bearing the guilt of the entire world in His own body and rising from the grave on the third day. Take note of the awe-inspiring description of our Lord in Revelation 19:11-16:

> Now I saw heaven opened, and behold, a white horse. And He who sat on him was called Faithful and True, and in righteousness He judges and makes war. His eyes were like a flame of fire, and on His head were many crowns. He had a name written that no one knew except Himself. He was clothed with a robe dipped in blood, and His name is called The Word of God. And the armies in heaven, clothed in fine linen, white and clean, followed Him on white horses. Now out of His mouth goes a sharp sword, that with it He should strike the nations. And He Himself will rule them with a rod of iron. He Himself treads the winepress of the fierceness and wrath of Almighty God. And He has on His robe and on His thigh a name written: KING OF KINGS AND LORD OF LORDS.

This is our Jesus—the ultimate man, the ultimate King. This is warrior-poet manhood. Jesus is greater, mightier, stronger, and more powerful than anything our minds can comprehend. In the face of such spectacular majesty, how can we possibly think, *Jesus was a softie, therefore we should be too*? Christ was the ultimate blend of strength and sensitivity. He rules the nations with a rod of iron, and yet He is the Prince of Peace. He fiercely commands the winds and waves to obey Him, and yet little children find sweet refuge in His arms. He is the ultimate warrior-poet. And, as it says in 1 Peter 2:21, He left an example that we should *follow in His steps*. This applies to masculinity. It is the example of Christ—not the culture—that men are to follow. Jesus was anything *but* a metro male. And it's time we start calling men to the standard of our King.

Eric writes an imaginary movie scene in his book *The Brave-hearted Gospel* that paints a great picture of what happens when the manly stuff is robbed from masculinity. Imagine an old black and white movie scene in which a strong, handsome cowboy and beautiful young woman are tending to a mortally wounded horse. They both love the horse, and it is heartrending to hear the creature's agonized cries. It's time to make the tough decision to end the pain. What if the beautiful young woman, a bow in her hair and a feminine blush on her cheeks, were to grab the shotgun and say to the cowboy, "Carl, we are going to have to put her down." And then picture rugged cowboy Carl, in dusty leather boots and worn jeans, jumping in front of the horse and sobbing, "No, Jane! You can't shoot Trixie. You just can't!" He throws his body on top of the horse and weeps as the beautiful young woman stands her ground. "Carl, it's best for Trixie. If you really love her, you will let her go."

What's wrong with that picture? As Eric writes, "It just doesn't seem appropriate for Carl to be such a sap, and it seems strange for Jane to be so unfeeling. In a general sense, there is a way that we know men should be and there is also a way that we know women should be. And whether it's politically correct to acknowledge or not, the truth is we all instinctively know what falls under the banners of feminine and masculine behavior."[9]

As odd as the above scenario seems, men like Carl, who forsake their traditional manly roles and behave like soft-hearted women, are applauded nowadays. Having the old-fashioned idea that Carl should act like a real man and shoot the horse is an unpardonable sin. That's the result of metro manhood.

It's not just men who visit beauty salons and tanning booths who are affected by the "feminized" masculinity we see all around us. Our culture says that a man's intrinsic desire to sound a war cry and charge into battle is unsavory, undesirable, and socially incorrect. Our culture looks down upon a man taking a firm stand for truth and making the hard choices like shooting a dying horse. As a result, we are hard-pressed to find any men who actually fight battles or stand for anything. Instead, they sit on their couches playing Halo and watching action movies while this dying world perishes for lack of real-life valiant warriors. Our marriages languish because men aren't standing up and actually being men.

What would have happened if the author of that men's book I mentioned earlier had actually demonstrated warrior-poet manhood by fighting for his marriage? At the first sign of any danger to his marriage, he would have heroically and aggressively risen up to protect and defend the most important relationship in his life. Instead of nursing his own self-pity and pining after other women, he would have done whatever it took to fight for the preservation of his relationship with his wife. His prayer wouldn't have been:

Jesus, please help me before I do something stupid. Rather, it would have been: *Jesus, I call upon the power of Your mighty name. Infuse me with heavenly strength to battle for my marriage. I refuse to allow the enemy any access to this sacred marriage covenant. I won't stop fighting until there is absolute victory in this situation. Following Your lead, may I lay down my very life for this woman I have pledged my heart to.*

I guarantee the ending to *that* story would have been a triumph—not mediocrity.

What if that adulterous pastor from the church in our area had stood up and fought for his marriage rather than selfishly catering to the desire of his sinful flesh? What if the moment the enemy entered in and planted his twisted thoughts—*You deserve some time away by yourself. Your wife doesn't understand your needs and maybe you can find someone better*—that pastor immediately fought back with truth, love, and selflessness and did whatever it took to end the siege upon his marriage? Instead of fighting the battle, he rolled over and played the victim to the enemy's schemes, and the result was the loss of his marriage, family, and ministry.

One day I was setting up an outdoor party for my friend. Struggling to carry all of the party food, drinks, and other things from the car to my destination, I dropped several items and noticed two young men playing basketball. After my third trip back to my car, it saddened me to think that as they watched me struggle, it didn't even cross their minds to offer assistance. I am not sure if they were afraid I might be offended if they offered their assistance, but whatever their reason, it saddened me to realize gentlemen are no longer the rule but the exception.

—Ashley, 24

Too many men don't know how to be real men. They don't know how to fight. And they don't know how to heroically protect women. They've been "metro-ized" without even realizing it.

Just this afternoon, I received a letter from a woman who is married to a military man. Though he knows how to employ battle tactics out on the field, at home he is nothing but a helpless weakling. He sits at his computer all day long, ignoring his wife and children and allowing his family to fall apart.

Today's metro men desperately need an infusion of the mighty masculine strength that heroically fights to preserve and protect the things that are most valuable to God. As my friend Nathan says, "Men have lost their backbone and strength, their willingness to fight and protect and serve." That's metro manhood in a nutshell.

Animalistic Manhood

On the other end of the spectrum are the aggressive, domineering, animalistic men who use their masculine strength to conquer women rather than protect them. This is the kind of man who views women as nothing more than sex objects, existing for men's animalistic gratification. And unfortunately, this version of manhood is even more prevalent than weak, effeminate metro males. I took an informal poll of a number of godly young men from all around the country, asking them to describe the state of modern manhood. Overwhelmingly, the "animalistic" description was used. Here's a brief sampling:

> The typical male views women as objects for self-gratification rather than human beings. Men view women through a glass of lust. Women are no longer persons to be upheld, honored, and cherished, but rather, they are objects to be seen, touched, and talked about. I seriously think men (if

they can be called such) see women as simply existing to make them feel good.

—DAVID, 22

Too often guys go into a relationship only concerned about what they are going to get out of it. Their goal is not to serve and protect but, rather, to loot and pillage.

—TIM, 21

Masculine strength has been warped into superiority and domination. We see abusive husbands, fathers, rapists, and murderers coming from this twisted masculinity.

—JEREMY, 20

It used to be an honor to walk a young lady to her door after a nice night out. Now a date is considered a complete disaster if the guy does not make it to her bedroom (this, of course, after taking her to see the newest Ben Stiller flick and out to Applebee's for dinner). Men will be ridiculed and mocked if they do not excel in the game of "Masculinity" (which is now just another word for cheap sex). The current movies, music, and literature all point to the same verdict concerning the credentials of a "real man"—a young stud who is good in bed.

—RICH, 24

Metro men (though most are just as sex-obsessed as the rest of the male population) are *denying* their masculinity altogether. Animalistic men are *redefining* masculinity to mean conquering and debasing women to gratify their own sexual pleasure. While metro manhood warps the poet side of masculinity into a sappy feminine version, animalistic manhood twists the warrior side into a caveman-like, sex-obsessed version of masculinity. Both counterfeits stem from the same root problem—selfishness. Men, just like women, have bought into the age-old lie that "it's all about me!" And when it comes to sexuality, there is nothing that twists, warps, and perverts God's original intent more than that attitude.

Two weeks ago, I was invited to be a guest on a talk radio show, which turned out to be a podcast of two guys spewing horrific obscenities and pornographic sex jokes and trying to shock me with their graphic and perverted language. After I hung up on them, my first thought was, *Who actually listens to that slime?* But then I realized that's just how far modern manhood has fallen. The fact that two grown men can make a living spouting sexual filth all day long proves that animalistic, sex-obsessed men are absolutely everywhere. We all know that the pornography industry is booming, and most of us have picked up on the fact that lust, rape, sexual abuse, and adultery are running rampant in this country. To most women, it seems that nearly every man they encounter is defeated by sexual sin. Is that a mere assumption, or is it actual fact? When I polled that handful of godly young men mentioned previously, I asked them to be honest about how widespread the issues of lust, pornography, and perversion truly are. Their responses confirm our worst suspicions:

> It is an all-consuming wildfire.
> —BOBBY, 24

It is flat-out everywhere.
—JEREMY, 20

～～～

Only one in a hundred men are free from it.
—TIM, 22

～～～

Lust and sexual perversion are "normal" and any hint of the opposite (for example *not* lusting or looking at pornography) is abnormal, strange, and means there must be some "problem" with that individual.

—NATHAN, 23

Just like metro manhood, it's very clear that animalistic manhood has crept into the church. Christian men are ensnared by the very same perversions as their secular counterparts. All of the young men I talked to said unequivocally that their Christian guy friends are just as addicted to lust and perversion as their non-Christian friends.

This is why most Christian women don't think they can expect anything better. This is why countless young women lower their standards and allow themselves to be treated as little more than sex objects. They have given up on the idea that heroic, valiant, noble warrior-poet men really exist.

It's important to note that sexuality isn't the only area affected by animalistic manhood. Animalistic manhood boasts a complete lack of nobility and honor, and it glorifies caveman-like behavior— guys who freely belch, scratch, snort, and give off foul odors; guys who lay on their couches guzzling beer and grunting at the TV; guys who collect bathroom jokes and find uncanny pleasure in talking about anything and everything debased. Metro manhood can be a bit subtle as it twists masculine nobility, but there is nothing subtle about animalistic manhood. Animalistic men are the opposite of the gallant knights women dream of—and they're proud of it.

Crude behavior has become the new cool—even among Christian men. I can't even count the number of pastors I've encountered that have begun to lacquer their sermons with profanity. The more shocking and undignified they can be, the better. To be a "real man" now means being able to talk about cow manure in graphic terms from the church pulpit. A few weeks ago, my husband, Eric, was riding in a car with two Christian guys who began to let off foul odors and joke about it. They saw it as nothing more than "guys being guys." When Eric told them that their lack of dignity now was preparing them to have a lack of dignity toward their future wives, they were shocked. "You mean you don't do that stuff in front of Leslie?" one of them asked. Eric told them that he seeks to treat me with nobility and honor in every area of life—not making bodily noises in front of me, not leaving the bathroom door open when he is in there, not chewing with his mouth open, and so forth. He was just speaking of basic respect, but the concept riveted the attention of these two young men. They had never even heard of such a notion.

Nobility and honor have become things of the past. Chivalry is lost. Men don't open car doors for women or take them to romantic restaurants. They don't send flowers or love notes. They sit around telling bathroom jokes, cussing and burping, counting down the minutes until they can finally get a woman into bed with them.

Of course, there are plenty of animalistic guys who are smart enough not to wear their caveman-like attitudes on their sleeves. A guy with any amount of common sense has studied the female mind enough to know that a woman is turned off by a burpin', scratchin', grimy-tee-shirt-wearing slob and that he is far less likely to conquer a feminine heart (and body) with that kind of behavior. So rather than being open and boastful about his true intentions, he cleverly cloaks his animalistic desires behind a metro-like front—playing a purposeful game of sensitivity and social polish until a woman lets her guard down enough to give him what he wants. It's not true chivalry. It's merely a temporary restraining of the grosser elements of a man's nature to gain a woman's attention. As my friend Rich describes it: "Men on the prowl for their next girlfriend view themselves as a hunter and the woman as a deer. He sits and waits for the first 'deer' that comes into sight. He studies it, tracks its every move, learns how to act around it, and tries not to scare it off until the moment finally comes to seize the deer, capturing it as his own. For most men, finding a woman is about the hunt. The actual deer is just a bonus. In the end the hunter part of them comes out again, and soon it's time to find another deer."

A large majority of church-going young men play the game of "sensitive Christian male" to conquer women. Though they might follow the Christian pattern to build relationships, too many of them see marriage not as an opportunity to love and cherish a woman's heart, but as the chance to finally have their sexual desires met. Sadly, many young brides find out too late that the man they married has been putting on the act of Christ-like nobility only to unveil his true nature after the wedding day.

God has placed a warrior instinct deep within the masculine soul—the intrinsic desire to wage war, fight, and conquer. But animalistic manhood uses a man's "conquering" side only to fight for his own selfish pleasure and gratification. Instead of being valiant conquerors for the kingdom of Christ, animalistic men use their warrior instinct to vanquish purity, destroy innocence, and ruthlessly wipe out all that stands in the way of their own agenda.

As we discussed earlier, Christ is a valiant mighty warrior—a majestic rider on a white steed, waging war against all the powers of darkness. He calls His men to become mighty like Himself; to be strong, valiant, and heroic. Just look at this description of God's mighty men from Hebrews 11:

> And what more shall I say? For the time would fail me to tell of Gideon and Barak and Samson and Jephthah, also of David and Samuel and the prophets: who through faith subdued kingdoms, worked righteousness, obtained promises, stopped the mouths of lions, quenched the violence of fire, escaped the edge of the sword, out of weakness were made strong, became valiant in battle, turned to fight the armies of the aliens (Hebrew 11:32-34).

True warriors for Christ are unstoppable. They possess a superhuman strength fueled by the Spirit of God. Just like Christ, they gallantly vanquish all that stands in the way of God's glory. They do not fight and claw for their own selfish lusts. They defend, protect, and fight for the purposes of their King.

Almost every young woman I've ever talked to feels a certain measure of suspicion toward guys, even Christian men that seem to be upright. In our modern world, it is completely normal for men to be constantly "on the prowl" for women, looking for ways to conquer a woman's purity, ravage her heart, and leave her wounded and bleeding. As a result, women feel the need to protect themselves. Guys are guilty until proven innocent. Women are forced to assume that men are selfish, lust-consumed sex addicts who are only after one thing until they somehow prove themselves otherwise. But sadly, few of them actually do.

Wendy Shalit wrote a book called *A Return to Modesty* in which she contends that there is more to being a woman than becoming a mindless, emotionless sex object. She says that women naturally desire a romantic relationship rather than a one-night stand and that girls shouldn't be ashamed of wanting something more than casual hookups with guys. When thousands of young women responded enthusiastically to her message, choosing to esteem marriage over meaningless sex, *Playboy* magazine called it "A Man's Worst Nightmare."[10]

That's animalistic manhood in a nutshell. Instead of applauding and protecting a woman's desire for purity, romance, and true love, animalistic men see these things as threats. After all, if a woman actually wants to be loved and cherished before she agrees to have sex, think of how much longer it's going to take to get her into bed. If a woman actually wants to be married before she "gives in," that means a man has to relinquish his lifelong ambition of sleeping with hundreds of women. So, fueled by a warped warrior mentality, animalistic men mock, ridicule, and fight against the very things they were created to honor, preserve, and protect.

The fairy tales aren't stories about women staving off sex-obsessed men or nursing broken hearts from guys who stole their innocence. They are stories about valiant knights who rescue fair maidens and *give their lives* to protect the maidens from harm. It's every woman's dream to be heroically protected and defended by a strong and noble man. But in our world, women must protect *themselves* from the very ones who were meant to stand up for them. We must now be on guard against the very ones our feminine hearts were designed to trust and lean upon.

When God builds men into true Christ-like warriors for His kingdom, women finally gain the heroic advocates they have always longed for. True warriors *protect* purity rather than conquer it. True Warriors *fight* for innocence rather than scorn it. True Warriors *honor* women rather than debase them. They don't describe a woman of purity as "A Man's Worst Nightmare"— they honor, admire, and respect her. When true warriors emerge, women feel secure and protected—both from outside harm *and* from the fear of a broken heart. When true warriors are built, fairy tales become reality.

CHAPTER TWO

Warrior-Poet Manhood

what Christ-built masculinity really looks like

We are all too familiar with counterfeit masculinity. Most of us haven't seen many, if any, examples of the real thing. And if we don't take a step back and really examine God's plan, purpose, and design for masculinity, then we are likely to accept the modern-day version of manhood as the most we can ever hope for. Sure, it might not be a fairy tale, but that's life. At least he's a nice guy, goes to church, makes a half-hearted attempt at holding the marriage together, and puts the toilet seat down. That's better than nothing. In fact, it's light years beyond what most women have.

But is it God's *best*? Is it what He intended for *you*, His precious daughter, from before the foundations of time?

God created a man to *cherish* his wife (both before and after marriage), honor her, and delight in her all the days of his life. Our feminine longing for a fairy tale was actually put within us by our Maker because He desires to fulfill it—first through our

romance with Him and then through an earthly love story with
a true warrior-poet, if His plan for us is marriage.

The entire Bible is a picture of a beautiful romance between
the Bridegroom and His bride. The way our heavenly Bridegroom
treats His bride is the pattern for how a man should treat a woman.
He laid down His very life to rescue His beloved. Here's just a brief
sampling of the divine beauty, tenderness, and romance Christ lav-
ishes on His bride:

> Therefore, behold, I will allure her, will bring her into the
> wilderness, and speak comfort to her (Hosea 2:14).

> He brought me to the banqueting house, and his banner
> over me was love (Song of Solomon 2:4).

> Your gentleness has made me great (2 Samuel 22:36).

> Listen, O daughter, consider and incline your ear, forget
> your own people also, and your father's house; so the King
> will greatly desire your beauty, because He is your Lord,
> worship Him (Psalm 45:10-11).

> How fair and how pleasant you are, O love, with your
> delights! (Song of Solomon 7:6).

The divine dignity, beauty, and romance that Christ expresses
in His passionate pursuit of us are the very qualities He intends

to build in male and female relationships. His ways are even more perfect than the fairy tales. And we should expect nothing less when we've given our lives to Him.

Our heroic Bridegroom does not take counterfeit manhood lightly. He *condemns* men who treat women with dishonor, disregard, and disrespect. And He *commends* men who treat their wives as treasures to be cherished and adored:

> The LORD has been witness between you and the wife of your youth, with whom you have dealt treacherously; yet she is your companion, and your wife by covenant (Malachi 2:14).

> Have you not read that He who made them at the beginning "made them male and female," and said, "For this reason a man shall leave his father and mother and be joined to his wife, and the two shall become one flesh"? So then, they are no longer two but one flesh. Therefore what God has joined together, let not man separate (Matthew 19:4-6).

> Drink water from your own cistern and fresh water from your own well. Should your springs be dispersed abroad, streams of water in the streets? Let them be yours alone and not for strangers with you. Let your fountain be blessed, and rejoice in the wife of your youth. As a loving hind and a graceful doe, let her breasts satisfy you at all times; be exhilarated always with her love. For why should you, my son, be exhilarated with an adulteress and embrace the bosom of a foreigner? (Proverbs 5:15-20 NASB).

God created marriage—and everything leading up to it—to be a picture of heaven on earth. He created men to be a picture of the heroic manhood of Christ. He wants no less for you. No matter what the culture says, He is asking you not to settle.

But do real warrior-poets really exist anymore? That's the desperate question burning in the heart of nearly every young woman I meet. And I can say unequivocally that they do—because I'm married to one. Is Eric the *only* one? (That's the next urgent question that arises.) And I can say unequivocally that he is not—because I've had the privilege of interacting with scores of them around this country, and I am encountering more of them all the time.

So what exactly is a warrior-poet?

A warrior-poet has made a sacred covenant with his holy King. He has chosen to deny himself, take up his cross, and follow Christ. He no longer lives to please his own selfish desires. He lives to please his Lord. He is not seeking to draw attention to himself but to draw all eyes to Jesus. As John the Baptist said, "He must increase, but I *must* decrease" (John 3:30). That's the motto of the warrior-poet's life.

When I was first getting to know Eric, I saw a marked difference between the way he treated me and the way almost every other guy on the planet did. For one thing, he wasn't pursuing the opposite sex. He was pursuing Christ. The majority of his time was spent in prayer, in biblical study, and in serving God's kingdom on the mission field. In spite of his dynamic personality, he never sought to gain applause or be the center of attention. He didn't seek out attractive young women. Rather, he sought out the loners and the outcasts; those whom no one paid attention to. At a party or church get-together, he would often spend his entire evening in the corner, encouraging someone that everyone else had overlooked. Money had no hold on him. While other young men his age pursued success and wealth, Eric gave his money away and depended upon God alone for provision. I vividly remember one time when a money-hungry, multilevel marketer cornered Eric and asked him what kind of car he dreamed about driving. Eric shrugged and said, "I just need a car that runs." The salesman was stunned that Eric wasn't pining after a BMW like every other college-age guy he knew.

Eric didn't flirt—with me or any other girl. He'd made a commitment to honor and respect his future wife. Even in his friendships with girls, though he was friendly, he was careful not to draw their hearts toward him. He was set apart—first for Christ and then for his future wife.

Not long before I met him, God had taken Eric through a process of laying down every "idol" in his life. In college he'd been in a premed program, at the top of his class. In the midst of all his forward momentum, God asked him to lay down his money and career pursuits and give his life to the mission field. Eric's obedience caused many raised eyebrows among his peers—but his spiritual life went from mediocre to vibrant in a matter of weeks. He was extremely athletic—a soccer player and weightlifter. He was an impeccable dresser—always wearing the absolute latest styles. He was popular without even trying to be—elected homecoming king in both high school and college. God asked him to lay those things at the cross of Christ and even be willing to appear a fool to the world for the sake of the One who gave everything for him. Instead of leaning upon his own strength, prestige, style, appearance, or personality, he learned to lean on Christ alone.

It was Eric's willingness to lay down everything for Christ that shaped him into a warrior-poet. As he laid down all worldly allurements and learned to love his Lord with all his heart, soul, mind, and strength, he became a mighty, valiant, loving, compassionate man of God. No longer was he just a church-going, self-focused male with a Christian label. He was radically abandoned to the King of the universe—and every area of his life exuded the glory of Christ.

Every time I was around Eric, I found that afterward I was not thinking about Eric Ludy. I was thinking about Jesus Christ. Often after spending an hour or two listening to him passionately talk about the Word of God, I ended up in my room with my Bible, eagerly pouring over the Scriptures and seeking to know Christ more. Unlike anyone I had ever known, Eric Ludy drew me closer to Jesus. In fact, his example was a key factor in my own decision to live a radically surrendered life for Christ.

Although I am sometimes disappointed by male behavior—such as when guys walk by someone who is clearly in need of help and don't offer assistance or when they refuse to stand up for what is right—I believe there are a lot of guys out there who desire to be mighty men of God but have few examples and little encouragement from the women in their lives. I believe great men will rise up in our generation as we pray for them and give them the encouragement and opportunity to do so.

—Melanie, 28

There are lots of guys that demonstrate Christian qualities at first glance, but in reality they fall far short of the warrior-poet standard. Before Eric's radical surrender to Christ, he would have come across as a wonderful, passionate, godly young man. He was committed to saving sex until marriage. He was committed to living an upright life of hard work and integrity. He was polite and well-mannered. He didn't drink or do drugs. His language was clean.

But *self* still ruled his existence. He wasn't consumed with Jesus Christ. He was consumed with selfish desires. Though he was governed by Christian morals, his life was built around the pursuit of worldly attractions and allurements—pursuing money, success, and the applause of men. He was the typical Christian male. Most Christian girls would have seen him as an amazing catch. But God had so much more in mind regarding his masculinity. And I thank God every day that Eric was willing to stand up and answer the call of Christ.

Christian young men are a dime a dozen. There are even many that seem to be a cut above the rest when it comes to their Christian values. But Christian values aren't the ingredients that make a true warrior-poet. A true warrior-poet emerges only when a man makes the decision to *lay down self* and *take up Christ.* Not to just say a sinner's prayer and accept the forgiveness of his sins, but to exchange *his very life* for the indwelling life of Jesus Christ and let all of his own dreams, desires, pursuits, and pleasures be swallowed up in an all-consuming passion for the Prince of his soul. As Eric says,

> Majestic man-ness is nearly extinct in our modern world. The version of Christianity most commonly espoused today is one that never sets a knife to the throat of self and says, "It's time for you to be going." The command center within the soul of a man is allowed only one ruler. If that ruler is self, then it cannot also be the true King of the universe. Who we choose as our ruler defines the substance, the quality, the character, and the eternity of our manhood.[1]

As I said before, I have the privilege of knowing many true warrior-poets-in-the-making all around this country. They are men who have relinquished self and taken up the cross of Christ—men who are not seeking to draw attention to themselves but to the King of all kings, men who are not in pursuit of the opposite sex but have made Christ the Lord and Lover of their soul, men who are not chasing after worldly allurements but are following hard after Christ.

A lot of young women complain to me that, while they might take my word that warrior-poets do exist, they never *see* any men like that. This is largely because true warrior-poets cannot be found amidst the throngs of typical Christian males. As I wrote in my book *Authentic Beauty:*

> Christ-like warrior-poets aren't usually mixed in with all the other mediocre males. They are living set-apart lives, just as our Prince has called us to do. They aren't often found in the normal crowds at typical guy-girl hangouts. They don't seek the spotlight. They aren't in hot pursuit of girls; they don't try to satisfy their loneliness with relationships. Christ-like warrior-poets are found on their knees in hidden retreats with their King or on the battlefield of human service or in diligent study of their Lord's ways.[2]

And as I have said before, the best way to find a Christ-like warrior-poet is to stop searching for one. Focus on your intimate love-relationship with Jesus Christ, and He will be more than faithful to bring a Christ-built man into your life in His own perfect time and way. It's amazing how God brings like-minded men and women together when we actually step back and give Him the chance to work.

Many young women ask me how high their standards for a guy should be. Is a warrior-poet one who *perfectly* reflects the manhood of Jesus Christ? What if there are still evidences of selfishness or immaturity in his life? Does that mean he's not the real thing?

The mark of a warrior-poet does not lie in his *perfection,* but in the *direction* of his life. Is he aiming for the world or aiming for Christ? Is he eagerly pursuing more of Christ or is he preoccupied with himself? If his life's direction is pointed toward "less of me and more of Him," then he has the warrior-poet blood within his veins, even if God has not yet rasped and refined all the rough edges of his masculinity. If he has made Christ the center of his existence, then Christ will be faithful to smooth away the wrinkles and refine him more and more into His divine likeness.

Set-apart women, take heart—Christ-built warrior-poets *do* exist in today's world! In fact, you have a very important role in raising up even more of them. We, as women, are not helpless victims to the discouraging trends of modern manhood. If we are willing, we can actually become instruments of change and allow God's Spirit to work in and through us to convert mediocre men into the triumphant knights whom we've always dreamed of.

CHAPTER THREE

Unlocking Your Feminine Power

shaping the course of modern masculinity

Earlier this year when Eric and I were having dinner with a group of Christian friends, the conversation turned to how guys in the younger generation were disillusioned with God. After discussing the dilemma for a few minutes, someone turned to me and asked, "Leslie, what about girls? What would you say are young women most disillusioned with?" To me the answer to that question is obvious. Today's young women are primarily disillusioned with *guys*. Girls grow up reading the fairy tales and dreaming of Prince Charming. But by the time we get to sixth grade, we are presented with a standard of masculinity so shockingly below our ideal that we can't help but become disillusioned—and even dismayed.

As I said in a previous chapter, the disillusionment seems to grow more complete the older we get and the more men we encounter. I can count on one hand the number of young women I know who *haven't* had their heart broken and abused by at least one guy by the time they reached college. And even more disconcerting, only a small percentage of the married women I know are not completely disillusioned with their marriage. A Christian book for women says this on the back cover:

> You once dreamed of a life of Prince Charmings and fairy-tale endings. But now that you've grown up and arrived at womanhood, those dreams seem so far out of reach. Your husband isn't quite the guy you thought you married...[1]

What a sadly accurate portrayal of most Christian women's lives! The fact that books like this are becoming increasingly popular reveals that women have given up trying to do anything about the decline of chivalry, gallantry, and heroic manhood. We've shrugged our shoulders and accepted the dismal fact that fairy tales are nothing more than childish, unrealistic dreams. So we sit around in discussion groups trying to cope with our disappointing reality.

But what if we *can* do something about it? What if fairy tales really *are* possible? What if we aren't supposed to settle for such a dim outlook on love and romance?

As women, we have a far greater power over the course of masculinity than most of us realize. We can use our femininity to influence men toward strength or toward weakness. Unfortunately, most of us don't use our feminine power correctly. We nag, criticize, complain, manipulate, and seduce—hoping that our self-built techniques will somehow work some magic and turn a frog into a prince. But when *selfishness* is our motivation for changing guys, we only end up fueling the problem and leading men into even greater weakness. Just like there are counterfeit versions of masculinity, there are counterfeit forms of femininity—twisted imitations of God's original design for womanhood. Sadly, most of us are very well-practiced in the counterfeit versions. Let's take a closer look at some of the most common ones.

Arrogant Femininity

Back to that dinner conversation I mentioned earlier. When I told the group that I felt that young women are disillusioned with guys, I got an interesting reaction from the young men around the table. "I'm so sick of hearing that!" one of them spat angrily. "You can't even turn on the radio these days without hearing women bashing men. Every TV show is all about the brilliant woman looking down on the idiotic guy! How is a guy supposed to show-case a different standard when every woman he meets has already labeled him a lazy, selfish, stupid pervert?"

Though this man's reaction was a far cry from the warrior-poet standard, I had to admit that his words did have an element of truth to them. Our feminine culture in general has attempted to cover their wounded feminine dreams with an arrogant, haughty disdain for all modern men. Too many of us have adopted the "all guys are idiotic pervs" slogan and have eagerly bought into our culture's current trend of "men-bashing" jokes and attitudes. Not long ago I watched a man moving a heavy box as a woman next to me remarked dryly, "That's the only thing that men are good for, you know." It's a cultural joke that is completely accepted—anything that puts men down and builds women up is deemed funny, clever, and true. Guys are expected to grin wryly and agree with any statements posed against their masculinity or even par-ticipate in the "men being lower life forms" campaign. Of course, if a man ever put a woman down in a similar way, he'd be publicly tortured and executed.

Arrogant femininity is a form of self-protection. We don't know how to deal with the disappointment of modern manhood, and so we choose to cover our emotions with scorn. I have been in numerous conversations in which married Christian women sat around drinking coffee and bashing their husband's idiotic behavior—laughing and joking with the "all men are jerks, so we might as well get a few laughs out of it" attitude.

But arrogant femininity only traps men in their weakness. Once a guy has been labeled as a self-serving pervert, a lazy burper-scratcher, or a mindless, grunting caveman, he has very little motivation to become anything different. I have talked to many single guys who have told me, "What's the use in trying to change? Women will always see me this way. If I try to be noble, women won't appreciate it anyway. They'll just assume I'm faking it to get what I want." Married men can easily fall into the same trap, asking why they should bother trying to be different if their wives are going to always see them as unromantic, self-focused slobs.

All too many men, who would have otherwise risen to a higher standard, have become stymied and paralyzed by the attitude of women who don't believe they can ever change.

No matter what disturbing trends we see in modern manhood, the worst thing we can do is participate in our culture's scornful bashing of masculinity and label men as sex-consumed perverts or lazy slobs who will never change. That arrogant attitude only creates guys who shrug and say, "Well if that's all she thinks I can be, then why would I bother trying to be anything different?" But when women actually *believe* that men can become the heroic warrior-poets that they were meant to be, we cause guys to actually *want* to change.

God calls us to *respect* and *reverence* masculinity, not to scorn and bash it.

> Let the wife see that she respects her husband (Ephesians 5:33).

~~~

> ...the incorruptible beauty of a gentle and quiet spirit, which is very precious in the sight of God. For in this manner, in former times, the holy women who trusted in God also adorned themselves, being submissive to their own husbands, as Sarah obeyed Abraham, calling him lord (1 Peter 3:4-6).

Many a married woman has found that when she actually stops disdaining her husband and starts *respecting* him and *believing* in him (whether he deserves it or not), he is motivated to emerge out of his selfish stupor and actually become worthy of the respect she is offering him. (Note: This does not apply to physical abuse. In that case, remove yourself from the situation and report him to the proper authorities!)

The same principle applies to unmarried women. If you want the guys to start acting more heroic, don't label them, scorn them, or bash them. *Believe* that they can become something more. It's not having faith in a *man*, but in what our mighty, amazing, triumphant *God* can do *in and through* a man. Let your words bring life and encouragement, not sarcasm and disdain.

> [The tongue] is an unruly evil, full of deadly poison. With it we bless our God and Father, and with it we curse men, who have been made in the similitude of God. Out of the same mouth proceed blessing and cursing. My brethren, these things ought not to be so (James 3:8-10).

~~~

> For three things the earth is perturbed, Yes, for four it cannot
> bear up: For a servant when he reigns, A fool when he
> is filled with food, *a hateful woman when she is married,*
> and a maidservant who succeeds her mistress (Proverbs
> 30:21-23).

Arrogant femininity is not Christ-built femininity. It's a twisted
counterfeit of our feminine power—using our words to paralyze
and defeat men rather than set them free to become valiant warrior-
poets. As women, we are created to *build men up,* not tear them
down. This doesn't mean we lower our standards and accept mediocrity. Rather, it means that we motivate guys to rise up to the
standard of Christ through words and attitudes of *encouragement*
instead of disgust.

Nagging Femininity

The book of Proverbs says twice that it is "better to dwell in a
corner of a housetop, than in a house shared with a contentious
woman" (Proverb 21:9; 25:24). And again in Proverbs 21:19 it says
"it is better to dwell in the wilderness, than with a contentious
and angry woman." I don't know why we, as women, seem to
intrinsically think that criticism and nagging will change a man.
Guys don't often take our subtle hints that we want them to act
differently, so we feel the need to turn up the volume to get them
to wake up and smell the coffee. But the problem is that this is
a self-built solution to the problem. It's a twisted counterfeit of
true femininity. No amount of criticism or nagging will cause a
man to become the heroic warrior-poet of our dreams. In fact, as
Proverbs clearly shows, it will only drive him away from us. Most
guys *would* rather live in the wilderness or the corner of a housetop

than with a woman who is constantly griping, complaining, and angrily criticizing his manhood.

In my marriage with Eric, I have noticed that when I yield to my selfish desire to complain or criticize, all I do is tear down his masculinity, discourage him, and dampen his desire to change. But when I choose to keep silent and diligently *pray* about the weaknesses I see in him, God gently opens his eyes to the areas that need to be rasped and remade—and he willingly submits to God's refining work without a word from me. As women, it is not our job to change men. Only God can do that. Our job is to participate with God in bringing His desired change about—not through angry words or self-effort, but through diligent prayer and a Christ-like example.

> Wives, be submissive to your own husbands so that even if any of them are disobedient to the word, they may be won without a word by the behavior of their wives, as they observe your chaste and respectful behavior (1 Peter 3:1-2 NASB).

The same principle applies to single women. As we allow the Spirit of God to transform us into radiant examples of Christ's love, guys will be transfixed rather than turned off by our behavior and attitude. They will be won over to the ways of Christ simply by observing the beauty of Christ that exudes from us. A nagging or criticizing spirit quenches the power of Christ's Spirit within us, but a quiet, prayerful, reverent spirit brings true Christ-built feminine beauty to the forefront. When guys come face to face with stunning Christ-built feminine radiance, they can't help but evaluate their own behavior in light of it.

The next time you are tempted to nag, criticize, or complain about a guy's behavior, pray for him instead. Ask God to transform him, rescue him, and shape him into the mighty warrior-poet God intended him to be. Remember that God is not limited by a guy's weaknesses. His transforming power is far greater than any human sin or weakness that resides in a man's life. Ask God to build your faith in His mighty ways—and remember that He is *even more interested* in rescuing that guy's soul than you are.

Seductive Femininity

In this era of sex-obsessed masculinity, all too many young women have fallen into the trap of seductive femininity. We are taught by the culture from a very young age that the only way a woman can be considered beautiful is if she becomes sensuous and sexually aggressive. Most of us grow up believing the lie that the only way to be approved by guys is to become as much like a Victoria's Secret vixen as we possibly can. Instead of using our feminine power to motivate guys toward purity, we fuel the problem of lust and sexual perversion by catering to men's debased sexual desires. Proverbs 7 describes the ways of a seductive woman.

> And behold, a woman comes to meet him, dressed as a harlot and cunning of heart. She is boisterous and rebellious, her feet do not remain at home; she is now in the streets, now in the squares, and lurks by every corner. So she seizes him and kisses him and with a brazen face she (speaks) to him (Proverbs 7:10-13 NASB).

This woman is physically aggressive toward guys, sensually dressed, always "on the prowl" for men, and uses strategic flirting and manipulation to lure guys into her seductive power. She is careless of her purity and her heart, and she looks to male approval to bring her pleasure. Sound like anyone you know? I'm guessing the answer is yes because her description fits the majority of young woman in our modern culture, even most Christ-professing ones. It is considered normal for a young woman to be aggressive, flirtatious, and sensual toward guys and use her feminine allure to manipulate the opposite sex. But what does God say about this kind of woman?

> Do not let your heart turn aside to her ways, do not stray into her paths; for she has cast down many wounded, and all who were slain by her were strong men. Her house is the way to hell, descending to the chambers of death (Proverbs 7:25-27 NASB).

Wow. I'd say it's time we start taking our interaction with the opposite sex a bit more seriously. As set-apart women, we are called to reflect His lily-white, radiant beauty and not a hollow sex-appeal of our own making. Every single one of the godly young men I interviewed for this book said that they wished young women would begin using their feminine power for good and not harm, especially in the area of seduction and sex appeal. Countless Christian young women are dressing and acting far more like the seductive woman in Proverbs 7 than the radiant, dignified, beautiful woman of God in Proverbs 31. And in so doing, we are only causing guys to sink deeper into the pit of twisted sexuality and animalistic manhood. Just take a look at what a few Christ-built young men had to say about today's women and their seductive power.

> I often hear young women saying that they want a noble, heroic man who won't treat them like a sex object. These girls are making those statements in a tight miniskirt with a see-through tank top that is, well lets just say, a little bit more

than revealing. A woman is supposed to be mysterious, and that is one of the reasons why a man is drawn to her. When a woman exposes her curves to a man, it leaves little room for him to think about anything other than, well…sex. A Christian male will be more attracted to a woman's heart and soul than the curves of her body. Women cannot just complain about the lack of wholesome men in the world. We need wholesome women as well. When we see an uncompromising conviction in the standards that women have, we will start to see the standards that men have begin to change as well.

—RICH, 24

Just this week in the youth group that I lead, I found several young females wearing clothing (in weather that usually requires coats, hats, and maybe scarves) that was beyond inappropriate. Low cut tops, short shorts, and tight shirts are all simple clothing items that can be changed, not only to help guys but also protect and honor the women themselves. Further, things like teasing (with sexual innuendo), provocative looks, and suggestive conversations are not honoring and quite destructive.

—NATHAN, 23

The typical modern girl has lost all sense of propriety. Whether it's the way she dresses or the way she acts with guys, most boundaries have been removed. Girls wear clothes that draw the eye to their bodies in some way (too tight, too short, lines/designs that accentuate body parts). Girls are very comfortable with flirting and teasing. Girls talk about once taboo "girl" topics candidly with their boyfriends or guy friends. And all of these things open up new avenues for lust and impure thoughts.

—Tim, 21

~⌒~

Women, craving attention and affection, have bought the lie we fed them that if they want us to notice them, then they'd better flaunt what they've got and be willing to satisfy our sexual appetites. Therefore, attire shifted, as did behavior. We told them to flaunt, so they flaunt. We told them to satisfy, so they satisfy. It has gotten to the point that we, as men, now expect such behavior. Even a man seeking to pursue purity is now hammered with images that constantly assail their desire for purity. A guy can't even walk down a mall corridor anymore without having to constantly avert his eyes.

—Jeremy, 20

Most of us continually justify our seductive behavior, thinking that as long as we are a cut above Paris Hilton, we are being modest and dignified. Our culture's standards for feminine purity have sunk to a nonexistent level. We all too often compare ourselves to the perversion that's all around us and assume we are doing pretty well if we walk the beach in anything more than barely-there string bikini. And, as long as our teasing and flirting is a bit tamer than a Christina Aguilera video, we think we are living wholesome lives. But what is God's standard?

The unmarried woman cares about the things of the Lord, that she may be holy both in body and in spirit (1 Corinthians 7:34).

~⌒~

> But she who lives in pleasure is dead while she lives (1 Timothy 5:6).

～～

> The women adorn themselves in modest apparel, with propriety and moderation, not with braided hair or gold or pearls or costly clothing, but, which is proper for women professing godliness, with good works (1 Timothy 2:9-10).

To be holy in both body and spirit is to be the entire focus of our lives. Not to be a step or two above the world's twisted ways, but to be completely separate from the world (in dress, actions, and attitude) and completely set-apart for Christ. This is not just a decision to wear a one-piece swimsuit instead of a bikini or a slightly longer miniskirt than what is currently fashionable. Rather, it is an *entire shift* of lifestyle and focus. It's allowing the very Spirit of Christ to enter into our being and transform us into pictures of purity from the inside out.

> Or do you not know that your body is the temple of the Holy Spirit who is in you, whom you have from God, and you are not your own? For you were bought at a price; therefore glorify God in your body and in your spirit, which are God's (1 Corinthians 6:19-20).

We cannot glorify God by flirting, flaunting our body, or using our seductive power to win the approval of guys. We don't draw attention to Christ through selfish manipulation and sex-appeal—that only draws attention to ourselves and brings guys down. If we want to see a positive change in the animalistic attitude of today's men, it's time we stop catering to the problem. It's time we begin to live as if we *actually are* the holy temple of the Most High God.

Controlling Femininity

> And I do not permit a woman to teach or to have authority
> over a man, but to be in silence. For Adam was formed first,
> then Eve. And Adam was not deceived, but the woman
> being deceived, fell into transgression (I Timothy 2:12-14).

Scriptures about women being silent and allowing men to lead can easily make us squirm. Our fleshly, selfish side gets uncomfortable at the idea of yielding complete control to Jesus Christ, and it's that same selfish voice that balks at giving men a higher position of leadership and authority. It's ironic. We long for men to rise up and become valiant warrior-poets worthy of our honor and respect. But often the moment we see a man start to emerge into a strong leader, all too often we feel threatened instead of encouraged. We start using our feminine power to manipulate, control, and keep him under our thumb. We want men to be strong. But not if it means we have to give up our own position and control. This is especially true in romantic relationships. I've encountered many a young woman who has become quite skilled in keeping her man under her thumb. She uses her beauty, her wit, her intellect, her personality, and her emotional power to control and dominate the guy in her life. She shapes her man into the man *she* wants him to be rather than allowing him to become the man God wants him to be.

For a guy to become the warrior-poet God intends him to be, he must be set free to *be a man.* In a marriage that means he's allowed to be the leader. He's given the position of final decision maker. It means that his wife allows him to guide and direct their relationship, their family, and the spiritual climate of their home. That does not mean that the woman has no say in any of these areas. On the contrary, a woman's input and influence in a marriage and family are crucial parts of God's design. Whenever a woman is told to "get in her place" and given no voice whatsoever, that's a very clear sign that things are grossly out of balance. However, when a woman usurps authority over a man, diminishes his voice, and manipulates him into doing everything her way, that's an equally unhealthy picture.

A marriage that is truly a picture of heaven on earth is one in which the man is fully yielded to Christ and the woman is fully yielded both to Christ and to her husband. In my marriage with Eric, we approach life as a team. When there are decisions that need to be made, he doesn't just haul off and make them without me. Rather, we sit down together and share our individual perspectives, pray together, and come to a place of complete unity before moving forward. But if there is ever a situation in which Eric feels strongly about something that I don't completely agree with, I allow him to be the final voice. I find that, as I submit to his authority, he does not gain a power trip from it. Rather, he honors and respects my opinion all the more.

Here is a recent example. When we were in the process of adopting our daughter, Harper, from Korea, we found out that she might have some medical problems, such as slow brain development. Conventional wisdom told us to take her medical file to a doctor to find out the extent of what we might be dealing with. I found that I was anxious to know more about her possible problems and told Eric I thought we should research them. But after praying about it, Eric said he felt it would be far better to simply trust God and pray—rather than jumping the gun, having her file examined, and labeling her as having medical problems before she even arrived home. At first it was hard for me to yield to his desire—my "always be prepared" attitude resisted the idea of just waiting and praying. But after a couple of weeks, God had filled my heart with such an overwhelming peace that Harper's health was completely in His hands, I no longer felt the need to rush out to a doctor for advice. Eric felt strongly that Harper would be perfectly healthy when she arrived home. Sure enough, that's exactly what happened. I realized that if I had taken her file to a doctor, I would have likely spent months worrying about potential health problems that didn't even exist. And instead of her homecoming being the joyous celebration that it was, it would have been marred with concern and stress.

As I have submitted to Eric's leading in areas such as these, he gains greater respect for me. He honors my thoughts and opinions because he realizes that I am willing to allow him to be the final decision maker. If there is ever something I am particularly concerned about, he always takes it seriously when I bring it to his attention. I have strong input into his life—but my input comes from a heart surrendered to Christ and not merely from trying to push my own whims and agendas.

Even in a marriage in which the husband is not yielded to Christ, a wife can gain great spiritual ground by respecting his position and allowing him to lead (unless submitting to his leadership means violating the Word of God). Ephesians 5:22 says, "Wives, submit to your own husbands, as to the Lord."

As you prepare for marriage, you can begin to put this principle into practice in the way you relate to guys. In friendships or in romantic relationships with guys, be cautious about using your spiritual insights or convictions in a controlling way. Too many young women fall into the trap of looking down on guys who don't share their same level of spiritual maturity. If there is a guy in your life who seems less spiritually mature than you, don't rub that fact in his face. Rather, be humble in your interaction with him, knowing that God is the one who must grow and build his faith, not you. Be an example of Christ to him, encourage him, cheer him on in his pursuit of God, and pray diligently for him—but don't spiritually manipulate him.

Not long ago, Eric and I encountered a young dating couple in which the girl was clearly dominating the guy. His words, actions, and decisions were completely controlled by his girlfriend. His identity became completely swallowed up in her, to the point it seemed he hardly had his own thoughts, ideas, convictions, or personality. How did the girl gain such control in their relationship? Two words: spiritual manipulation. She acted like she had a special ability to hear the voice of God, and it reached such a point that her every whim, thought, and emotion was presented as something that "God had spoken to her." The guy was intimated by this and assumed that she had a much closer connection with God than he did. He began to listen to his girlfriend's voice and treat it as the voice of God. She was more than happy to let him follow her around like an obedient puppy and loved the sense of control that it gave her. But fast-forward a few years down the road, and this relationship will be found in shambles. God designed a man to be the leader and the woman to honor that position. When God's pattern is violated, we lose the beauty He intended romance to have, and we invite a world of tension, stress, turmoil, and heartache into our lives.

It may be hard on your fleshly, selfish side to give up control and let a man take the lead. But in the end, it's far more romantic. After all, what girl dreams of being a gritty, iron-fisted princess who rescues a trembling, wimpy, weak-minded guy from the dragon, carries him away to her kingdom, and tells him exactly how to think and act from that day on? Doesn't sound much like happily-ever-after material to me! In our hearts, we don't want a "yes, dear, whatever you say, dear" kind of guy. We want a strong man who we can admire and respect. So let's not rob men of their masculinity in a childish battle for control.

Women have an incredible power to shape the direction of masculinity. In fact, it is largely women who are responsible for the wimpy, weak, slothful version of manhood we see all around us today. When women became obsessed with pushing the feminist agenda, we pushed men behind the scenes and forced them to take a backseat to our methods and opinions. We made it socially deplorable for a man to take a strong leadership position or even try to be a gallant, heroic gentleman. When Eric first arrived at his Christian college and tried to hold the door open for a young woman, she snapped at him and reprimanded him for his outdated male chauvinism. When he commented in one of his classes that he felt men should protect women, he was mocked and corrected by the professors and students alike. He quickly got the message that being a gentleman, or a strong masculine leader, is tantamount to being a Nazi. Feminism has swept every corner of society, destroying true manhood in its wake. I find it so ironic that the very thing that women desire most in men is the very thing they are militaristically fighting against. Don't get me wrong. I'm not against women having equal rights with men or women being a strong influence in politics and the work force. But when women begin to dominate men, take over a society, and become so arrogant that we won't allow men to be men, the result is the twisted mass of dysfunctional male and female dynamics we see all around us today.

In the same way that women can have a negative influence on the course of manhood, we can also use our feminine power to *restore* masculinity to the way God intended it to be. You may not feel that you can make much of a difference, but if you allow the Spirit of God to make you a vessel for shaping future warrior-poets, you'll be surprised at how many lives will be forever changed. God used one young, insignificant shepherd boy named David to remove all that stood in the way of Israel's glory.

Hudson Taylor was just a slothful, self-focused teenager when his sister and mother began praying intensely for his soul. The influence of two devoted women shaped Hudson into one of the greatest and most heroic missionaries of all time—impacting countless thousands with the gospel of Christ and motivating countless Christians to step out and fulfill the call of Christ with unwavering courage.

John and Charles Wesley were just ordinary boys who were shaped into heroic princes by the tireless example and prayers of their mother, Susanna. As a result they changed the face of Christian history and brought the power of God to a wayward generation.

Richard Wurmbrand was transformed from a hesitant pastor to an unstoppable force in God's kingdom by the exhortation and encouragement of his wife. He stood boldly against the Communist regime, suffered in prison for 14 years, and became the international voice of the underground and persecuted church.

Don't underestimate what God can do through one young woman who stands for His ways. Warrior-poets can be awakened in this generation. So why not let the revival begin with you?

CHAPTER FOUR

Heroic Womanhood

practical ways to shape men into princes

For a full picture of what a true, Christ-built woman looks like, I would highly encourage you to read my book *Set-Apart Femininity.* But for the sake of comparison to the counterfeit versions of femininity that we've just discussed, here is a brief snapshot:

> God's sacred intent for us goes far beyond just saving sex until marriage, wearing one-piece swimsuits instead of skimpy string bikinis, or idolizing Christian bands instead of secular ones. It is not just making sure we tack on some Christian morality to our self-indulgent lives.
>
> His sacred intent for you and for me is nothing short of absolute abandonment to Jesus Christ, entire separation from the pollution of the world, and ardent worship of our King with every breath we take.

Yes, it's a huge vision—one that is contrary to everything our culture presents. In our modern world, we as young women seem to be presented with only two options for our femininity—we can either embrace the sensual, sexed-up version of womanhood glorified by pop culture or we can go the opposite direction and trade in perfume and makeup for grit, grunge, and guy-like behavior.

But both of these options cause us to completely miss out on the glorious pattern God designed for our femininity. We were created to shine with heavenly beauty, to radiate with Christ-like feminine loveliness, and to sparkle with the lily-white purity of our Prince. We were created to be set-apart for Him.[1]

When we finally become consumed with Jesus Christ alone, allowing Him to reign and rule over every dimension of our femininity, we will become the spectacular, radiant, and truly beautiful women whom Godly young men dream about. When we are passionately in love with our heavenly Prince instead of passionately pining after the approval of worldly men, we will have the kind of femininity that can truly shape the course of modern manhood. This may surprise you, but there are just as many godly warrior-poets out there wondering if any set-apart young women exist as there are girls wondering if Christ-built guys exist. In the same way that I have to constantly remind girls that godly warrior-poets are really out there, I have to reassure guys that Christ-consumed young women aren't as rare as it might seem. Warrior-poets are longing for the emergence of set-apart young women—women who are not afraid to stand for something more than the culture's mediocrity. Women who aren't afraid of being labeled uptight, prude, or stiff. Women who are completely unconcerned with what the world thinks of them because they are entirely caught up in the glorious reality of Jesus Christ.

Christ-built femininity is a force to be reckoned with. When we allow the purity and power of Almighty God to radically transform our entire approach to womanhood, the men of our culture will step back in wonder. Every godly guy I've ever talked with has told me that when he encounters a young woman who is wholly consumed with Jesus Christ, she captivates him far more than even the most beautiful supermodels ever could.

Real-Life Application

It's surprising how many Christ-focused young women I meet have a difficult time transferring their romance with Jesus into the arena of guys. We might accept the fact that Jesus Christ is a princely, heroic gentleman who laid down His very life on our behalf. But when it comes to guys, we quickly settle for a self-consumed, arrogant guy who only uses us to get what he wants— guy who puts on a Christian mask to gain our attention, but underneath he is no different than his non-Christian counterparts. As I have said in many of my previous books, an earthly romance is meant to be an *outflow* of our heavenly romance with Christ. A human love story was designed to be a *picture* of the stunning romance between Christ and His bride. The only way this can happen is for both individuals to be completely consumed with Jesus Christ—to be ruled and operated not by selfish motives, but by His divine Spirit alone.

Just the other day, my coworker told me about a potential date opportunity. "Kelly, he is absolutely perfect for you!" she said excitedly. Trying to keep myself composed, my mind was already forming a mental picture of what this future date looked like. I blushed, thinking of how great this guy just might turn out to be! It was then that I realized I was missing a very important piece of information. "Well, is he a Christian?" I had to ask.

My coworker rolled her eyes. "Kelly, it's just one date. It's not like he has bad morals or anything. Just go and get a free dinner and then see what happens from there. You could always ask him to church or something over dinner."

I shrugged and thought about it. Is just going out for a dinner really such a big deal? I could always witness to him, right? What if this was God's way of getting him to come to church?

This is the type of thinking that gets us all in trouble. I know from experience. One of the greatest rules of thumb is if an action requires justification, run! The allure of dating is strong in our culture. But if you have learned to cultivate a love relationship with Christ, His love is more alluring than all else. When I looked through the eyes of Christ at "it's just a dinner" opportunity, I saw nothing more than an imitation of what Christ desired. It was a fake substitute and a distraction to the real thing.

Christ did not die so that we would suffer as victims to our flesh. He died so that His life in ours would give us victory, joys inexpressible, and peace beyond all understanding. This is the life that Christ has called us to. Anything less, like dating a non-Christian, is simply compromising and rejecting the life that Christ came to give!

—KELLY, 24

Hold Out for God's Best

There are lots of Christian guys out there—guys who profess Christ but allow *self* to reign and rule their lives. Just because a guy is friendly, clean-cut, polite, and church-going doesn't mean that he is a true warrior-poet. All too many young women lower their standards out of desperation, thinking that if they don't snag the one guy who seems at least somewhat better than the rest, they will end up alone. But this attitude demonstrates a complete lack of trust in God's good and perfect plans for your life. If you give Him the pen and allow Him to script your story, you don't need to strive or manipulate to make a romance happen. He will bring the perfect guy into your life in His own perfect time and way. God is more interested in this area of your life being beautiful than even you are!

If you settle for less than a man who is fully yielded and surrendered to the King of all kings, you settle for less than God's best for you. You may not feel worthy of a noble, gallant, Christ-built warrior-poet who will lay down his life for you, but this is exactly what Christ is to you. And this is exactly what He desires for you in an earthly prince. If you keep your standards high, you honor Christ. You acknowledge that you were purchased by the precious blood of Jesus, that you are the daughter of the Most High King, and that you will not cheapen all that Christ has done for you by throwing your pearls to a swine (see Matthew 7:6). Christ has made you into royalty. Do not throw that gift away by giving the treasure of your femininity to a self-serving pig.

How can you tell the difference between a Christ-built warrior-poet and a cleverly disguised self-built Christian man? There are many ways.

First, learn to listen to the voice of Christ's Spirit within you.

The more you diminish your own selfish voice and tune in to what His Spirit is whispering to your soul, the more you intrinsically sense when God is opening a door or when He is telling you to be cautious. If you need wisdom about a guy in your life, devote plenty of time to diligent prayer. The more you pray, the more clear God's voice will become.

And don't rush ahead because of impatience. If there is any doubt in your mind, it is always best to err on the side of caution rather than presumption. If God wants you to take a step forward with a guy, He is perfectly capable of giving complete peace and confidence to your soul. If there is uncertainty, the best thing to do is to wait and continue to pray until your path becomes clear. God will not allow you to miss His will if you simply build your life around seeking Him.

When I interact with guys, I've learned to maintain certain boundaries both physically and even in conversation. My goal is to protect both the guy and myself. I choose to keep physical expressions of affection sacred by waiting to enjoy them in marriage. I refrain from sharing the deepest areas of my heart with guys because I want to give my husband the honor of being the only one to gain access to that part of me.

—Courtney, 23

Second, spend time observing the guy "behind the scenes" when no one else seems to be watching. He might be a wonderful example of Christ when he is in front of his church friends, but what is he like around his family? How does he treat his younger siblings? Does he honor his parents? What is he like around the "unlovable" people—those who can't do anything for his reputation or popularity? Does he seek the limelight, or is he content to be in the background, ministering to those whom everyone else overlooks? What is the overall direction of his life? Is he pursuing money, or is he truly pursuing Christ? Does his "spiritual wisdom" come from hours on his knees alone with God or merely from what he borrows from the spiritual lives of others? Is he truly respectful of women and honoring to his future wife, or is he constantly trying to win the affection of girls? Take some time to quietly observe his behavior (over more than just a day or two!) and allow God's Spirit to open your eyes to his true nature.

Thirdly, recruit some "teammates" who can observe him along with you. Often the best teammates are parents or godly older adults you respect rather than friends your own age who might just tell you what you want to hear. Your parents (if they are walking with Christ) have been given a special position in your life by God, and often they have special insight into important decisions such as this one. If you are willing to humble yourself and submit to their wisdom, God can work through them to give you caution or assurance as you decide whether to move forward in a relationship. As I detailed in my book *When God Writes Your Love Story,* my parents played an incredibly important role in my love story with Eric. When our friendship seemed ready to move into a romantic relationship, their insight and wisdom proved to be an invaluable tool that God used to give me peace. Even if you are an adult and living completely independent of your parents, they can still serve as prayer partners and godly counselors for this crucial area of your life. If you are willing to listen to their perspective, you will be surprised at how beneficial it can be.

All of the godly young men whom I interviewed for this book agreed that if young women started keeping their standards high rather than settling for mediocre men, guys would be forced to make serious changes to their masculinity. And even if you are mocked, ridiculed, or ignored because of your stand, you can be sure that God will honor your decision. He paid for the treasure of your heart with His own blood. You disregard His amazing sacrifice for you when you allow your femininity to be trampled in the mud. You are a daughter of the King so hold out for a man who has *royal* blood coursing through his veins.

Let Him Win Your Heart

I have yet to meet a woman who dreams of a wimpy, insecure guy who has no clue how to lead or take the initiative in a relationship. But few women realize that when they steal a guy's position and become the initiator rather than the responder, they shape men into wimps, not warriors. Most of us are so eager for a guy's approval that we carelessly throw ourselves at anything male that looks our way. Among today's love-hungry women, a man typically doesn't have to work very hard to win a woman's heart and attention. In fact, often all he needs to do is flirt for a couple of minutes, and the next thing he knows she's completely given her heart, emotions, and even her body to him. Just like settling for less than a Christ-built man, throwing ourselves at guys cheapens the amazing work Christ has done for us. He gave up His very life to make us into His radiant princesses. Why would we take such a gift lightly by throwing our feminine hearts to anything male that moves? Our heart, emotions, innocence, and physical purity are treasures from heaven. These treasures are only to be entrusted to *one* man (our future spouse) and only *after* he proves he is truly worthy of such a gift.

Though most modern guys might appear to want women who are aggressive and easy to get, this kind of femininity is not what will capture the heart of a true warrior-poet. God designed men to diligently and valiantly *pursue* a woman. Guys are naturally intrigued by a woman with mystique—a woman who isn't willing to auction her heart and body to whomever passes by. If a man actually has to *work* to win a woman's heart, he will be far more likely to cherish and appreciate the gift he's labored so hard for. On the other hand, if a woman throws herself at him, though he might initially respond, he won't have much respect or appreciation for such easy prey, and he will never learn how to tenderly cherish the treasure of her heart.

As I said in my book *Set-Apart Femininity,* the entire Bible is a picture of the romance between Christ and His bride. He tenderly woos and pursues us, and when our heart is won over to Him, He loves and cherishes us as priceless treasures. Christ is the initiator, and *we* are the responders.

> We love Him because He first loved us (1 John 4:19).

> I have loved you with an everlasting love; therefore with loving-kindness I have drawn you (Jeremiah 31:3).

> Therefore I am now going to allure her; I will lead her into the desert and speak tenderly to her (Hosea 2:14 NIV).

The entire book of Song of Solomon paints a vivid picture of a man pursuing a woman's heart and then cherishing the priceless treasure he's worked so hard to win. If you want a truly beautiful romance with a valiant warrior-poet who will value the gift of your feminine heart, don't follow the easy-to-get trends of our modern

culture. Don't throw yourself at a guy out of impatience or desperation. The only man truly worth spending your life with is the one
who will diligently, tenderly, and nobly pursue your heart, proving that he is worthy of the treasure of your purity—the treasure
Christ Himself purchased on the cross.

So how do you let a guy win your heart? Here are a few practical tips.

Don't Be in a Hurry

So many young women I talk to feel that the moment a guy
shows interest in them, they are in an urgent situation and need to
make a quick decision. This exposes their desperation—their fear
that if they don't jump on a good opportunity, they'll miss their
only chance for true love. It shows a lack of faith in the Author
of romance. Remember that if His plan for you is marriage, He
is more than capable of keeping a guy's interest, even if it takes
months or years for you to finally give him the go-ahead. A man
who is truly worth his salt knows that you are worth the wait and
won't put pressure on you to make a quick decision. Jacob worked
for Rachel for *14 years* and they seemed "only a few days to him
because of the love he had for her" (Genesis 29:20). If God truly
desires a relationship to happen, you don't need to rush or feel
pressure to open the door to a guy. When a guy shows interest,
the first thing to do is spend an ample amount of time in prayer
and seek godly counsel. I don't just mean praying for a day or
two. I mean diligent, persistent prayer, seeking God's wisdom
and heart for the situation. Ask His Spirit to show you whether
this is truly His highest and best for your life. Remember that,
other than your decision to accept Christ, the decision of which
guy to marry is the most important decision you will ever make.

It will affect you for the rest of your life. It's not something to take lightly.

It is extremely dangerous to just experiment with relationships to see if you really like a guy or not, giving your heart to one person after the next in an attempt to find the right one. When God builds a relationship, He brings *one* man and *one* woman together for the rest of their lives. He is able and willing to guide you into His perfect plan *without* taking you through a handful of failed relationships and broken hearts. He is able and willing to write your love story in such a way that you give your heart to only one man—the man you will spend the rest of your life with. But most of us don't trust Him enough to allow Him to do that for us. We feel the need to rush into a relationship so that we don't lose a guy's interest. All too often, we end up brokenhearted and damaged. If there is a potential relationship in your life, the best first course of action is this:

> Trust in the LORD with all your heart, and lean not on your own understanding; in all your ways acknowledge Him, and He shall direct your paths (Proverbs 3:5-6).

If you slow down and take the time to really seek Him, you can be sure that He *will* direct and guide you. There is no reason to ever take a step forward in a relationship unless you have complete peace and certainty in your heart—a certainty not based on your own emotions but on hours of spending time in God's presence and seeking His heart and wisdom.

Recruit the Help of a Protector

In the olden days, a man would have to go to a woman's father and receive his permission even to "come calling" on her. In other words, he couldn't spend time getting to know her without getting the okay from her "protector." Culture has changed to such an extent that there is now a blatant disregard for the concept of a woman having any kind of protection or authority over her life. It's usually seen as archaic and oppressive for a man to actually honor the position of a woman's parents in the beginning of a relationship. But yet again, it's an issue of placing *value* on the priceless gift of your feminine heart. When you allow your parents (or other godly leaders) to serve in a position of protection over your femininity, you acknowledge that the treasure of your heart is precious to Christ and must be treated with the same dignity and respect that He gives to it.

A guy can prove he is worthy of your heart by *honoring* the people that have a position of protection and authority in your life. This doesn't have to mean a stuffy, old-fashioned process in which your parents sit between you and a potential suitor on the couch. Rather, it's simply asking your parents (or other godly leaders you trust) to serve as your prayer partners, counselors, and protectors in this area. They don't have to make all the decisions for you. But if you allow them to be involved—if you respect them enough to take their opinions seriously—you will receive an incredible blessing. If a guy knows that he has to go through your protectors to begin a relationship with you, he will take the whole process far more seriously. He is far less likely to use you and break your heart when he knows that there are eyes on him, looking out for your best interest. In fact, asking a guy to go through your protectors often proves what his motives truly are. If he shies away from sitting down and talking with your parents about his intentions, chances are he has something to hide. But if he willingly submits to their questions and scrutiny, very likely his motives toward you are pure and his feelings for you are strong enough that he is willing to get uncomfortable in order to win you.

Even if you are on your own, completely independent of your parents, it can be a wonderful idea to let them serve as long-distance protectors and prayer partners for the relationship. Or consider finding someone closer by who you know has God's heart for you. Recruiting protectors can feel awkward at first. But if you are willing to submit to the counsel and leadership of those God has placed in authority over you, you are far more likely to find real beauty and success in this delicate area of life. (If your parents are unable or unwilling to fill this role, consider recruiting the help of a pastor or godly spiritual mentor.)

In other books I have written about Eric's relationship with my dad during the development of our relationship. They met together regularly and talked about what God was doing between us, exploring ways that Eric could best honor me during the process. I never would have expected it, but this was one of the most *romantic* dimensions of my love story. What woman wouldn't feel like a princess with the two most important men in her life meeting together and talking about how to be sensitive and honor her? It was largely through submitting to my dad that Eric proved he was truly worthy of the gift of my heart.

Keep Sacred Things Sacred

Even after a relationship has begun, remember that there are certain things that are meant to be savored and kept sacred until the proper time. If you lay your entire heart and soul bare before a guy in the very beginning of a relationship, it takes all of the mystery and excitement away. Let him *discover* who you are—not all in one day, but over a longer period of diligent exploration.

Don't divulge all your deepest secrets, longings, fears, and desires right off the bat. Let God direct you in the gentle opening of your heart and gradual unveiling of the deepest treasures of your soul. Allow trust to build slowly and gradually. Share more of your heart with him the more he showcases the nature of Christ in his interaction with you. Allow him to *seek out* the inner workings of your heart. Maintain a sense of feminine mystery and guard the sacred things for sacred moments. This applies to both emotional guardedness and physical purity. Eric and I didn't hold hands until we knew we were in a relationship headed toward marriage. We didn't exchange the words "I love you" until the night of our engagement. And we didn't kiss until our wedding day. It may sound miserable and restrictive, but it was truly like a fairy tale. Because we kept sacred things sacred, it was mysterious, exciting, and beautiful—completely different than the careless, unromantic love stories so common in our modern times.

Following the narrow path of Christ-built femininity truly is hero work. It means choosing to live selflessly and sacrificially in order to help shape men into the princes God created them to be. Remember that God has not called you to walk this path in your own strength. If you submit your femininity fully to Him, He will give you everything you need to become a radiant, vibrant, heroic example of His nature. Even if you have been living far from the path of heroic femininity, Jesus Christ is ready to shape you into His likeness, starting today. So don't wait another moment before yielding to His perfect way. You'll never regret such a decision.

CHAPTER FIVE

Becoming a Princess of Purity

helping guys rise above sexual sin

The problems of lust, perversion, and sexual addiction can seem overwhelming when you take a look at the state of modern manhood. But there are plenty of practical ways that we as young women can help guys overcome the sexual pitfalls that are so prevalent in today's world. We must remember that society's sexual problems are not just a result of modern guys. Girls are huge contributors. We shouldn't just point the finger of blame at the opposite sex and sit around complaining about how many guys are sexually warped. Rather, we should diligently pray that the sexual climate of our culture would realign with God's pattern. And then, by His enabling grace, we should do everything that lies within our power to help that dream become a reality. Here are some practical ways we can begin.

Dress with Dignity

All the godly young men whom I interviewed for this book mentioned immodesty as a huge factor in the demise of modern men. Christ-built warrior-poets are longing for young women who will dress in a way that assists a man's mental purity rather than tempts him to compromise. But being a young woman myself, I know that you can't just say "dress more modestly" and leave it at that. I am well aware that this area is a huge challenge for modern Christian young women. Just a few months ago, I went to the mall hoping to find a couple of summer tops. After visiting ten stores and trying on countless possibilities, I walked away empty-handed. Much to my frustration, the only shirts available were tight, low cut, and see-through. And unless I wanted to shop in the grandma section, there seemed to be no modest options. As fashion trends become more and more sensual, most Christian girls feel they have no choice but to comply with culture. Dressing modestly (and fashionably) these days is an art form. Most of us aren't willing to go to the effort it takes to overcome the challenges and dress with grace, mystique, and dignity. Add to that our desire to be found appealing to the opposite sex, and we end up with dismally low standards for the way we dress. We know that we'll get more attention from guys in form-fitting tops, tight pants, and short skirts. And it's all too tempting to rationalize immodesty because "at least this outfit isn't as bad as a lot of things I could wear." We think that as long as we aren't going topless on the beach, we have an element of modesty. But what is God's standard?

> I want women to adorn themselves with proper clothing, modestly and discreetly (1 Timothy 2:9 NASB).

The word *modestly* literally means "with shame and bashfulness." In other words, not shamelessly flaunting our bodies, but exuding a sense of careful dignity and guardedness even in the way we dress. The word *discreetly* means "to keep hidden." A woman's body is for the enjoyment of one man alone—her husband. God asks us not to give other men the privilege of viewing what belongs only to the man we will spend the rest of our life with.

It's easy to assume that true modesty means drab, shapeless, unfeminine clothes that make us extremely unattractive. But God's pattern doesn't bring oppression and ugliness—it brings liberty and beauty. Contrary to popular belief, feminine beauty doesn't have to mean sensuality. It is more than possible to exude the kind of dignity, grace and true feminine beauty that will captivate a man's heart—without using sex appeal.

Don't think of modest dressing as a dour duty that leads to restriction and misery. Consider it a wonderful opportunity to showcase the stunning beauty of Christ, not the cheap counterfeit of feminine beauty espoused by the culture. It's the ability to capture the heart of a Christ-built warrior-poet by a feminine grace unseen in today's world. It restores the value and honor to femininity that every woman desires. And it challenges young men to treat women with true respect and decorum instead of seeing them as cheap sex objects.

We must remember that our bodies are not our own (1 Corinthians 6:19-20). Therefore, because our bodies house the presence of the living God, we cannot just assume that it is our right to do whatever we want with them. Rather, our body is to be spent for the glory of our King—not for the selfish pleasure of lustful men or to gratify our own selfish desire to be found attractive to the opposite sex.

In addition to our body being the sacred temple of the Most High God, our body also belongs to our future husband. As it says in 1 Corinthians 7:4, "The wife does not have authority over her own body, but the husband does." Therefore, we must consider our husband's feelings and *honor* him with our body, even before we meet him. The Proverbs 31 woman does her husband good and not harm *all* the days of her life, not just after she is married.

Living to honor Jesus Christ and our future husband *must* be our core motivation when it comes to dressing modestly. If we are asking the question "how much can I get away with?" we are considering our own selfish desires above the desire of Christ.

I've hesitated to give specific guidelines for dress in my previous books because I don't believe modest dressing can be made into a formula. Rather, we must be led by the Spirit of God. But because I've been asked by countless thousands of young women for some practical suggestions, here are some to consider.

Showing Skin

Here is the rule of thumb that works for me on where to draw the line regarding showing skin: Any area of my body that can be associated with sensuality is not to be touched *or* seen by anyone other than my husband. For example, if someone touches me on the elbow, there isn't anything sensual about it. In fact, often at weddings or fancy restaurants, an usher or waiter will take me by the arm and lead me to my seat. Eric has no reason to be concerned about this kind of interaction because there's nothing sexual about it. But if a guy came up and touched me on the thigh, it's a completely different story. Eric would have every reason to be jealous, angry, and hurt because touching someone on the thigh is definitely associated with sensuality. Any area of my body that would be awkward or uncomfortable for another guy to touch is an area of my body that I keep hidden for my husband's eyes alone. Chest, thighs, stomach—these might seem like harmless areas to show off, but if you were married and wanted to stay that way, you wouldn't allow another guy to touch you in any of those places. So why would you allow another guy to have the privilege of looking at what was meant for your husband's pleasure alone? When you keep your husband's feelings at the forefront of your mind when deciding what to wear, the issue of how much skin to show becomes far less complicated.

Showing Figure

Lots of young women I know frequently wear clothes that conceal almost every bit of skin on their body, and yet their outfits are anything but modest. Tight and form-fitting clothes can be just as sensual (if not more so) as clothes that reveal a lot of skin. It's really the same rule of thumb that applies in this situation. Any area of your body that can be associated with sensuality shouldn't be viewed by other men—whether by showing skin or by showing form. A turtleneck might not show any skin whatsoever, but if it is super tight, then you are leaving very little to the imagination for any guy who happens to look your way. The same goes with pants and skirts. They might cover every square inch of skin, but if they cling tightly to your figure, you are giving guys the pleasure of viewing what was meant for only your husband's enjoyment.

This is not to say that wearing tent-like dresses or baggy clown pants are your only option. There are many stylish and looser fitting pants that are feminine and flattering but don't "give away the farm." They may be hard to find in the teeny bopper stores at the mall where every pair of jeans is labeled "ultra-low-cut-stretch," but I've found that some of the "young professional style" stores have some pretty good options. You may have to pay a bit more for them, but it's better to have one or two pairs of classy, feminine jeans or pants than a whole closet full of super tight ones that only get tighter every time you wash them! Remember, even though you may get male attention by wearing form-fitting clothes, a true warrior-poet is longing for a woman who showcases the true beauty of Christ instead of the cheap counterfeit of the culture. If you dress to honor your future husband, then a warrior-poet won't have to avert his eyes when you walk into the room. You'll be like a breath of fresh air to his soul. He'll notice the light of Christ in your eyes and the radiance of your smile rather than being distracted by the outline of your body.

Dressing like a Lady

Once upon a time, women wore elegant, feminine clothes and carried themselves with dignity and poise. A man wasn't enticed by sensual, slutty outfits. Rather, he was captivated by true beauty and feminine grace. But "dressing like a lady" is a lost concept these days. Most modern girls either dress seductively or like slobs. The Proverbs 31 woman (whom I wrote about in great detail in my book *Set-Apart Femininity*) is the epitome of feminine beauty and feminine valiance. She is clothed in "strength and dignity." She makes coverings for herself of "fine linen and purple." She has the respect of her children and community and has captured the heart of her husband. When a young woman dresses with the grace and dignity of a true lady, she gains the *right* kind of attention from the *right* kind of guys. Don't think of modest dressing as giving up being feminine or attractive. Think of it as exchanging the culture's cheap counterfeit of feminine appeal for the stunning, *God*-designed version of female allure. Warrior-poet men aren't just looking for women who purposely dress down their feminine beauty or hide behind drab, tent-like clothes. They desire to see young women who exude a loveliness and graceful feminine beauty that flows from the inside out; a feminine dignity that is both modest and stunningly, refreshingly beautiful. Modest dressing isn't a mere obligation so that we don't cause guys to stumble. Rather, it's one of our most powerful tools in restoring respect, dignity, and nobility to modern femininity. Christa Taylor is a young clothing designer who said it this way:

> When a young woman chooses to dress in a way that thoughtlessly exposes her body or, worse, seeks to use her body to allure men sexually, she is reducing herself to mere "eye candy." All that is truly good and beautiful and unique about a young woman is lost and she is only seen as an object for sex. Womanhood today is so crude, largely because of the attack on female modesty. Many mainstream fashion trends are very unflattering. Low rise jeans, for instance, can create "muffin tops" and when seated, reveal way too much of your derriere to the unfortunate individual behind you. This does not enhance a woman's beauty or attractiveness. In contrast, a woman who is dressed with dignity and grace, in feminine apparel that flatters, draws attention to her face, her personality, and charm.
>
> Modesty is the ancient secret of allure. An oxymoron? I think not. When women choose to dress with modesty and dignity, it just might flip everything around...We were created in such a way that when we humans act without restraint and without any rules, we don't have as much fun! Modesty and dignity help women protect their romantic hopes, challenge men to be courteous and honorable, and will turn the whole sexual revolution on its head. That is something to look forward to.[1]

Swimsuits

Once upon a time, women's swimsuits actually covered the sensual areas of the body, and it was perfectly normal to swim with real clothing on. Now going to the pool or the beach means walking around in clothing that doesn't cover much of anything, which explains why modern men flock to swimming areas in order to lust after women. Walking around in modern swimwear is basically like walking around in your underwear. And while most of us wouldn't walk through the mall or go to the bus station in nothing more than a bra and panties, we think nothing of walking the beach in such a skimpy ensemble. We assume that because something is called a *swimsuit,* it means it's different than what comes out of our underwear drawer, despite the fact that it leaves the same amount of skin exposed. Even if you choose not to wear a two-piece, most one-piece suits are so form-fitting that they leave very little to the imagination. Nearly every modern swimsuit reveals areas of the body that are meant only for the enjoyment of our future husband. Sure, it's socially acceptable to walk around half-naked when you are near water. But does that mean we should just accept the cultural trend without a second thought? Most of us think that modesty guidelines automatically "loosen up" when it comes to swimming because it just seems unreasonable to cut out swimming altogether and it's impractical to swim in jeans and a tee shirt. But if we are seeking to dress with dignity in every other area of our life, why would swimwear fall into the "exception" category just because it might be a difficult area to navigate? As far as I am concerned, the same standards for modest dressing should apply to swimwear as to the rest of our wardrobe. If we are showing off parts of our skin or figure that are meant only for our husband, then we are not dressing as a set-apart woman.

I realize this presents a pretty significant dilemma, considering there aren't many, if any, stores that carry truly modest swimsuits. You'll probably have to get creative. For the past few years, I have worn "water shorts" over my swimsuit when I swim—loose-fitting shorts that are made to go in the water and that actually cover up the parts of my body I don't want seen. Because I used to race in triathlons, I discovered that there are athletic swim tops that are made for competitive sports rather than showing off the female body. I wear these kinds of swim tops when I go to the beach. I feel perfectly comfortable in them. No one thinks that I am trying to make a modest fashion statement, and I am free to enjoy the water without wondering if men's eyes are on me. A friend of mine swims in water shirts and shorts made for surfers that she orders from www.rashguardshirtco.com. Most companies that sell women's triathlon clothes carry racing shorts and tops that are made to go in the water but are far more modest than traditional swimwear. Christa Taylor (quoted above) launched her own clothing company for young women. Her line of clothing, including modest swim-suits, is available at www.christa-taylor.com. With a little research and effort, dressing with dignity and modesty can be achieved even in the area of swim clothes. Both your future husband and all the warrior-poets out there will be thrilled if you take the time to honor Christ in this area of your life.

Praise Princely Behavior

One of the greatest ways that you, as a young woman, can help change the course of modern masculinity is with your words. Just as the sarcastic put-downs of arrogant femininity or the relentless criticism of a nagging woman can prevent a man from rising to a higher standard, so Christ-shaped words of praise and encouragement can motivate, inspire, and rally a man to embrace the fullness of God's design for his masculinity. As it says in Proverbs 25:11, "a word fitly spoken is like apples of gold in settings of silver." Guys may not act like they need or want encouragement, but in reality, the life-giving words of a woman have a tremendous impact upon their heart. When a guy realizes that a woman notices and applauds him when he does something Christ-like, he is far more likely to want to cultivate and repeat that behavior. Even if a guy isn't quite up to warrior-poet standards, allow God to show you things in his life that *are* of a Christ-like pattern. Then let the guy know that you appreciate what you see in that area of his life. Chances are he'll start doing it more often. Plus, he'll awaken to the fact that he has the potential to be noble. Most guys just need to be told that they have princely attributes, and then they are more than eager to cultivate them. In the heart of every young man (especially those that have come to Christ) beats the desire to be truly heroic and honorable. Just as we desire a gallant knight to rescue us, guys desire to be a strong and noble rescuer. Most of them just don't know how. The words of set-apart women can go a long way in pointing them in the right direction.

Many girls ask me how to encourage a guy without coming across as interested in him. Your ability to inspire and encourage guys in a nonromantic way stems from the way you act around him the rest of the time. If you are diligent in guarding your feminine mystique, then even when you encourage a guy, he is not likely to get the wrong idea about your intentions. If you don't go out of your way to hang around a guy, if you don't engage in flirtatious banter with him, and if you don't giggle or grin at his less-than-Christ-like actions and words, you'll be able to freely encourage his positive attributes without coming across as interested. If you come across as strong and confident in your own femininity, you'll win a man's respect, and he'll take your words of encouragement seriously rather than as hints toward a relationship.

Obviously, the *way* you encourage a guy is important. Pulling him aside for an intimate one-on-one chat probably isn't the best strategy. Dropping him a quick, casual email that says, "By the way, I really appreciated how you reached out to little Kyle yesterday at church," is a safe way to go. Or if you want to encourage him right on the spot when you see him doing something noble, just take a quick moment to affirm him by saying something like, "What you just did was really a blessing to me—this world needs more guys who will take a stand like that!" or whatever seems appropriate at the time. Again, asking the Spirit of God to direct you is crucial. And don't limit your encouragement just to guys your own age. As I've said in other books, take the time to invest in your dad and brothers. You have a very important position in their lives, and your words of praise and encouragement can help shape them into heroic princes. Many a set-apart young woman has told me how her decision to speak words of life to her younger brother had a life-changing impact on his masculinity and prepared him to become the warrior-poet God intended him to be.

Get God's Heart Toward Lust and Pornography

When guys you know are controlled by lust and entrenched in pornography, it can be hard to know how to treat the issue. The modern church seems to go out of its way to tell women not to act repulsed, shocked, or disgusted by male perversion but, rather, to be understanding of the fact that this is a huge struggle for guys. We are told to be an encouragement and support to them. There is an element of correctness to this approach. As we discussed earlier, criticizing or scorning guys for their weaknesses will only push them away and convince them they can never change. However, we must remember how God views lust and sexual immorality. Does He simply offer guys a shoulder to cry on and say, "Don't worry, I understand that lust will always be a struggle for you—just know I am here if you ever need to talk"? Just the opposite! Christ said,

> You have heard that it was said to those of old, "You shall not commit adultery." But I say to you that whoever looks at a woman to lust for her has already committed adultery with her in his heart. If your right eye causes you to sin, pluck it out and cast it from you; for it is more profitable for you that one of your members perish, than for your whole body to be cast into hell (Matthew 5:27-29).

To Jesus Christ, sexual immorality is not just something to shrug off. It's not something a man is supposed to "always struggle with." God sees lust and sexual sin as disgusting and defiling. He is so passionate for a man's purity that He says it is better to enter heaven maimed than to allow the control of lust to lead a man straight to hell. If God is deeply grieved by sexual perversion, then as set-apart women for Christ, we should be too. We should never just pat a guy on the shoulder and say, "I understand this will be an ongoing struggle for you—and I'm here if you need to talk." Our hearts should *grieve* for our brothers in Christ who are so entrapped and ensnared by the controlling power of sin. We should long to see them completely delivered and set free, and we should *believe* that through the power of Jesus Christ, *they can be!*

Recently Eric confided to a Christian leader that years ago he had been set free from the controlling power of lust—not that he wasn't still vulnerable to the temptation, but that he was no longer *enslaved* to mental impurity. The Christian leader later mocked

Eric for pretending to have any kind of victory in this area of his life. "We all know that it's a joke to think that a guy could actually be free from the power of lust," he said. "Every Christian guy is controlled by lust—it's just part of being a man in a fallen world!"

If you have picked up on this defeated mentality toward men and the sin of lust, you are not alone. But it doesn't matter what today's Christians have accepted as normal. It only matters what Christ says. And here is what *He* says about victory over sin:

> Knowing this, that our old man was crucified with Him, that the body of sin might be done away with, that we should no longer be slaves of sin. For he who has died has been freed from sin. Now if we died with Christ, we believe that we shall also live with Him, knowing that Christ, having been raised from the dead, dies no more. Death no longer has dominion over Him. For the death that He died, He died to sin once for all; but the life that He lives, He lives to God. Likewise, you also, reckon yourselves to be dead indeed to sin, but alive to God in Christ Jesus our Lord. Therefore do not let sin reign in your mortal body, that you should obey it in its lusts (Romans 6:6-12).

> We know that whoever is born of God, does not sin; but he who has been born of God keeps himself, and the wicked one does not touch him (1 John 5:18).

One of the main reasons that so many Christian men are ensnared by lust is that no one believes or expects them to ever gain complete victory over it. Sure, there are support groups and Bible studies that focus on keeping the sin of lust "under control," but very few focus on annihilating it altogether. The Christian leaders who should be challenging them and exhorting them to a higher standard are themselves trapped in the same pit. So rather than saying, "Follow me as I follow Christ!" they say, "Follow me as I wallow in sin and defeat—it's okay, we are all in this together!"

So where does that leave us as set-apart young women? We have an important role to play. If no one else will call men to the standard of Christ, then it's time we fulfill the call. If there are men in your family or your life who are controlled by sexual perversion of any kind, you don't have to sit helplessly by and watch. Remember that "greater is He who is in you than he who is in the world." Christ has given us the mighty power of His Spirit—and that power is greater than the power of lust and sin. So how can we participate with Christ's Spirit in bringing victory to defeated masculinity? Here are some ways to begin.

Pray

When you see a guy stumble in sexual sin, don't waste time worrying about it, gossiping about it, or being discouraged by it. Rather, pour all of your emotion out to God in passionate, heart-felt prayer. In my book *Set-Apart Femininity,* we talked about the incredible power of importunate, persistent prayer. If anyone in your life, male or female, is defeated by any kind of sin, the very best thing that you can do to help them is commit to wrestle for their soul in prayer. Remember that the "effective, fervent prayer of a righteous man (or woman) avails much" (James 5:16). Your persistent prayers on behalf of another person will be heard, and they will make a difference. In fact, God may have opened your eyes to the struggle so that you can stand in the gap in prayer. If you won't cry out to God on behalf of a struggling brother, who will? You may be the only person in his life with enough passion and conviction to wrestle for God's perfect will to be accomplished in his life. Earlier this year, I prayed with several young women who cried out to God—with heartfelt weeping—on behalf of their brothers who were steeped in sin. A few months later, the girls began to see the fruit of their prayers. Their brothers each began to hunger after God and emerge from their sinful stupor. As it says in Galations 6:9 (KJV), "Let us not be weary in well doing: for in due season we shall reap, if we faint not."

Hate What God Hates

Yes, it *is* okay to be repulsed and shocked by pornography and sexual sin. In fact, if we *don't* hate the things that God hates, we don't possess the mind of Christ. You don't need to soften your response toward sexual sin to keep guys from feeling guilty or condemned. When young women finally begin to take a stand against sexual perversion, guys will be forced to take this area of their lives more seriously. Don't give into the pressure to just chuckle and shrug it off when a guy makes a sexual comment or talks about his lustful habits. Let your reaction state that you are *grieving* for his wandering heart. Whether you respond in silence (which can send a very loud message!) or make a quiet comment like, "I believe that you can be a better man that that," allow God's Spirit to direct your response. Make sure that you respond with the *love* of Christ and not just your own selfish anger or hurt. As it says in 1 Corinthians 13, love *believes* all things. Love doesn't just call a person on their sin and leave them there. Rather, love speaks truth and then *believes* in the power of God to set us *free* from sin.

Quite a few young women have written to me wondering

how to react when they catch their dad, brother, boyfriend, or guy friend looking at online porn. Just in the past few months, I've heard from several women who caught a man in the act of watching porn on his computer. "I am so upset to find out that my own brother is doing something like this! Should I just pray for him or should I say something to him?" a young woman named Kylie asked in a recent email. Again, this is something that *must* be directed by God's Spirit, and it depends on the individual situation, but here are a few guidelines that you might find helpful.

> *For brothers:* It is a good idea to go to your parents or someone else in authority, especially if your brother is still living at home. Don't think of it as ratting him out, but doing what is best for him because you love him. He will need to be confronted about his behavior, and *you* might not be the best person to do that. Take it to someone in a leadership position who can sit down with him and call him to a higher standard. Even if it creates friction in your family relationships or causes your brother to be angry at you for a while, most likely he will eventually come to see that you only want God's best for him and you love him too much to let him head straight off a cliff. If there is no one in authority whom you can take it to, you might consider sitting down with him and confronting the issue—but only after much prayer and following the Spirit's lead! Don't let anger or accusation direct the conversation. Rather, speak with the attitude that communicates how you want something better than this for him. Ask him how you can work with him to overcome it." Sometimes friction must be created

for healing and deliverance to begin. As it says in Proverbs 20:30, "Blows that hurt cleanse away evil, as do stripes the inner depths of the heart."

For dads: This can be a very sticky issue because most young women don't feel comfortable telling their moms that they just caught their dads looking at porn. They don't want to be responsible for the possible demise of their parents' marriages, which is completely understandable. Your first course of action, when you are dealing with your dad, is persistent prayer. If God directs you to discuss it with your mom, follow His lead. But He may just ask you to continue praying for deliverance. If there is a trusted, godly leader in your dad's life whom you can go to, then by all means, do. A trusted friend might be able to confront your dad's sin far better than you could because no dad wants to be put to shame in front of his daughter. If there is no one whom you can go to, then consider writing your dad a letter. It is usually best not to shock him or put him on the spot. A letter can get his attention, without you having to sit through an awkward or defensive conversation. But if you don't feel a letter will get his attention and there is no one else whom you can go to for help, a face-to-face conversation might be the right thing to do. Remember to let God direct and guide your words in love and not accusation. If you share a computer with your dad, don't hesitate to put on filters and blocks that make it more difficult for him to get to porn sites. These actions can often speak even louder than words, and at least he will have some measure of accountability.

For boyfriends: Sorry to be so blunt, but if you find out that your boyfriend is addicted to porn, it's time to end the relationship. I know that sounds a bit harsh, but remember that this is the season when a man proves what he's really made of. It's far better for you to end the relationship now than have to wake up one day and discover you are married to a man who lusts after other women. Don't string a lust-ensnared guy along in the hopes that he might eventually change. He might clean up his act for a while to keep you around, but unless he allows the Spirit of God to deeply penetrate the depths of his soul and remake him from the inside out, he is not a man who is worthy of your heart. In almost all cases, the best thing that you can do is respectfully end the relationship (not temporarily, but permanently) and allow *God* to resurrect it at some point in the future, if He chooses and only *after* the guy has proven that he truly has been made new in this area. You don't need to use criticism or accusation when you take this step. Simply say something along the lines of, "I feel that there is more work God needs to do in your life before you'll be ready for a Christ-centered relationship." Make sure that he knows you hope and believe that Christ will redeem him and make him new. He may lash out in defensiveness or anger, but eventually he'll realize that your actions were out of genuine Christ-like love and concern for his soul. It will force him to either embrace warrior-poet manhood or follow the mediocre trends of our day. If women don't start taking a stand and expecting more out of men, then the standard will never get any higher.

(Important note: An occasional stumble in the area of

lust is different than complete given-ness to its controlling power. If, after exploring the situation, you believe that your boyfriend is not ensnared by this sin but merely gave in to it momentarily, and if he has truly repented and is diligently seeking a life of real purity, then you may *not* need to walk away from the relationship. In fact, you might be an important influence in encouraging him to gain great accountability in this area of his life. However, be sure that he is not just telling you what you want to hear—that he is truly and passionately following after God's best for his life.)

For guy friends: Guy friends also pose a sticky issue because female friends don't always have an intimate position to speak into their lives on such a personal matter. However, you may be the only one who is willing to call them to a higher standard so don't just assume that someone else will do the job. No matter how awkward it might be, always put his soul above your concern for keeping the friendship. Maintaining your status as his friend is far less important than helping him become right with God and free from the power of sexual addiction. This is where tough love comes in. Do what's best for him, not just what's most comfortable for you. Usually the best thing that you can do is go to someone in a position of authority over his life and share what you know. Recruit the help of a pastor, godly father, or other Christ-like leader who can confront him and challenge him to address this area of his life. Make sure that you don't go to someone who won't take the issue seriously. There are plenty of male Christian leaders who might simply shrug it off and treat you as a naïve female for even being concerned. If you don't have a trusted man to go to who has God's heart in this area, then you may have to confront your guy friend yourself. Pray and ask the Spirit of God to equip you. Whether it is in a face-to-face conversation or a letter, let the guy know that you are concerned for the state of his soul and for the protection of his future wife, that you believe God can and will deliver him from the power of sin and make him into warrior-poet material, and that you will be diligently praying for him to have the grace to escape the slippery slope of pornography. Sometimes just knowing that a female friend is concerned for him is enough to motivate a man to take his decisions more seriously. Of course, he may become defensive and even distance himself from you out of a sense of embarrassment, shame, or conviction. If that happens, continue loving him, showcasing Christ consistently to him, and praying for him. Don't take his rejection personally. It's not about you. It's about the discomfort in his own soul. And don't underestimate the power of prayer. Often those who seem most "hopeless" are the very ones in whom Christ works most dramatically. Your love and concern *will* make a difference.

Guard Your Own Heart

Contrary to popular belief, lust and pornography aren't problems only guys deal with. They can entice and entrap women just as easily, if we are not on guard. Here are two exhortations from Scripture.

> Keep your heart with all diligence, for out of it spring the issues of life. Put away from you a deceitful mouth, and

put perverse lips far from you. Let your eyes look straight ahead, and your eyelids look right before you. Ponder the path of your feet, and let all your ways be established. Do not turn to the right or the left; remove your foot from evil (Proverbs 4:23-27).

~~~

Pure and undefiled religion before God and the Father is this: to visit orphans and widows in their trouble, and to keep oneself unspotted from the world (James 1:27).

To keep oneself unspotted from the world means to remain *completely* unstained by corruption and pollution. The more of the world's pollution we allow into our minds and hearts, the more susceptible we are to the entrapment of mental perversion and lust. In my book *Set-Apart Femininity*, I shared in detail about my decision to lean on God for my rest, refreshment, excitement, and joy instead of looking to the cheap counterfeit of worldly entertainment. Not only has this decision skyrocketed my level of intimacy with Christ and my spiritual growth, but it keeps my mind and heart meditating upon what is pure and holy rather than what is debased and perverted. Most young women I have talked to found that their first temptation toward lust or pornography came from movies, TV shows, or music they were exposed to. When we allow the warped mentalities of Hollywood to shape our perspective and fill our minds with impure images and attitudes, we open our minds wide for impurity to waltz right in and make itself at home. One of the best ways to guard your heart, keep yourself unspotted from the world, and remove your foot from evil is to eliminate worldly images and messages from entering your mind. This may sound extreme, but what does Christ say?

For whosoever will save his life shall lose it; but whosoever shall lose his life for my sake and the gospel's, the same shall save it. For what shall it profit a man, if he shall gain the whole world, and lose his own soul? Or what shall a man give in exchange for his soul? (Mark 8:35-37 KJV).

~~~

She who lives in pleasure is dead while she lives (1 Timothy 5:6).

Enjoying the temporary pleasures of worldly sights, sounds, and images isn't worth the pollution and corruption of our soul. Our goal should not be to constantly ask how much pleasure we can get away with and still remain on God's good side. Rather, like Mary of Bethany, we must pour out our entire lives upon His feet, without reserve. That is the kind of devotion that produces a pure heart and mind that brings glory to His name. We cannot change the course of modern masculinity if we ourselves are giving sway to lust and perversion. God calls us to be holy as He is holy. And He equips us by His Spirit to live the kind of sparkling pure and upright life that we could never live on our own. Prayerfully consider what avenues you are currently allowing into your heart and mind that glorify sexual sin and lust. Even if they seem small or harmless, there is no reason that anything of the kingdom of darkness should be allowed to remain in your life. If you haven't already, I'd strongly encourage you to read *Set-Apart Femininity* for an in-depth and practical look at the process of cleansing worldly impurity from every avenue of your life.

If you have become trapped in a pattern of lust or pornography, God wants something better for you. He is not looking at you in disgust and anger. He is gently and tenderly calling you to repent and turn from these sins. I would encourage you to take a focused period of time to repent of all impurity that has been allowed into your life, let God's Spirit wash your soul clean, and then purge every remnant of sexual impurity from your life. It can be extremely helpful to recruit a trusted accountability partner whom you can meet with regularly for prayer and support. And if you have godly parents, it's a great idea to confess your sin to them and ask for their help in purging these patterns completely from your life. I am a big fan of Internet filters and porn protection, as well as online accountability programs such as www.covenanteyes.com. Be aggressive and ruthless in removing all that stands in the way of God's fullness for you as His set-apart princess. Every step you take out of darkness and into His marvelous light will be more than worth it.

CHAPTER SIX

Code of Conduct

how to treat guys in everyday life

Countless young women have written to me through the years, presenting perplexing dilemmas about how to act around guys. In our sexually warped society, there is plenty of confusion about how to build a healthy guy/girl friendship, how to be friendly toward a guy without leading him on, how to deal with attraction toward a guy in a Christ-honoring way, as well as a myriad of other issues. Rather than reasoning after our own emotion or human wisdom, it's crucial to get in touch with *God's* heart on the subject of male/female interaction. He's the one who invented love and romance in the first place, so who better to turn to for counsel? Remember that He cares more about this area than even you do, and if you turn this area over to Him, He *will* be faithful to lead and guide you. His ways are not stodgy and miserable, but beautiful and life-giving. If you follow His design, you'll never regret it. So let's explore the heart of God toward some of the most common questions about relating to the opposite sex.

How do I get to know a guy in a Christ-honoring way?

Even in the get-to-know-you stage of a friendship, keeping Christ at the center is no less important than in a serious relationship. If there is a guy whom you feel drawn to get to know better, remember that the way you approach the friendship in the early stages can set the tone for the entire friendship and, if it ends up becoming more, the entire romantic relationship. For instance, many young women feel that the only way they can get to know a guy is if *they* initiate a friendship. "I don't know him very well, but I'm just going to call him and invite him to coffee. How else is he ever going to know that I am interested in having a friendship with him?" It sounds like a logical line of reasoning. But taking the initiative with a guy, even in the friendship stage, can be dangerous. God designed men to be the leaders, the initiators, and the pursuers in male/female relationships. Even if it seems harmless to ask a guy out to coffee or email him and let him know you want to get to know him better, it subtly undermines his masculinity. And as we discussed earlier, even though guys might at first seem to like it when girls pursue them, the reality is that when their masculine role is diminished, it hinders them from becoming the strong, confident leaders God intended them to be. The Bible says:

> But I suffer not a woman to teach, nor to usurp authority over the man, but to be in silence. For Adam was first formed, then Eve (1 Timothy 2:12-13 KJV).

When a woman takes a leadership role, even in a friendship, she subtly disregards a man's authority and position. To "usurp authority" over a man means to "govern" him. If you take the lead in a friendship or relationship with a guy, the weight falls on your shoulders to guide and govern the relationship from that point forward—completely backward from God's intent. You forgo the opportunity to be pursued and won by a heroic man. Rather than him proving that he is worthy of your heart, you now have to prove that *you* are worthy of *his*. How unromantic is that? As hard as it might be to wait for him to take the first step and reach out, you will be blessed for honoring God's perfect design. Even if the friendship never turns into anything romantic, by down-playing a man's role as pursuer, you are chipping away at his ability to be a Christ-built warrior-poet who will honor, serve, and protect femininity. Don't give in to impatience when you see a guy you are attracted to or interested in. Instead, take it to God in fervent, heartfelt prayer. If God desires the friendship to happen, He is perfectly capable of moving on the guy's heart to take the first step and reach out to you. Show that you trust in Him with *all* your heart by letting Him write the story without any manipulation on your part!

If there is a guy in your life you feel drawn to, honor God's design by reaching out to him in *subtle* and *Christ-honoring* ways, without undermining his position as the initiator. Here are some practical suggestions for getting to know a guy without sacrificing your femininity.

Engage in Christ-honoring Conversation

Protecting your feminine mystique doesn't mean you need to hide in a corner and go out of your way to avoid guys. It's not more spiritual to act shy and insecure in a conversation with a guy. You can be friendly, outgoing, and confident toward any guy you meet. The key is to be God-honoring in the *way* you speak and interact with guys. Scripture is abundantly clear that all our words must be carefully weighed before God.

But fornication and all uncleanness or covetousness, let it not even be named among you, as is fitting for saints; neither filthiness, nor foolish talking, nor coarse jesting, which are not fitting, but rather giving of thanks (Ephesians 5:3-4).

But I say to you that for every idle word men may speak, they will give account of it in the day of judgment. For by your words you will be justified, and by your words you will be condemned (Matthew 12:36-37).

Let no corrupt word proceed out of your mouth, but what is good for necessary edification, that it may impart grace to the hearers (Ephesians 4:29).

Let your speech always be with grace, seasoned with salt, that you may know how you ought to answer each one (Colossians 4:6).

Far too many of us get caught up in the playful banter that goes along with male/female interaction, disregarding the purity of speech that God requires of His children. When you casually chat with a guy, don't allow crude words, sarcastic words, impure words, profane words, sensual words, and gossipy words to creep into your conversation. Joking about the latest Hollywood comedy or TV sitcom might seem completely normal, but does it honor Jesus Christ? Flirtatious or teasing comments might seem innocent and fun, but does that behavior reflect the stunning purity of our King?

The other day I was among a group of Christian young adults who were having a casual conversation. One of the guys began to tell a story about how a woman had caught him with his fly open that day at work. At first it seemed like a funny, harmless story, but the descriptions and visual illustrations he used quickly put it into the "awkward" category. Even though the girls listening to him were passionate about purity and living a set-apart life, for the sake of social polish, they began laughing and joking with him—participating unwittingly in the "course and foolish jesting" warned against in Scripture.

You might feel uncomfortable remaining silent instead of laughing when a guy makes an inappropriate joke or comment. You might find it awkward to abruptly change

Treasuring the sacred core of who I am by not openly advertising the deepest places of my heart is really what adds mystique to my femininity. I allow my heart to be held, guarded, and cherished by my Creator! The closer I draw to Him, the more I long to protect that beautiful intimacy I share with Him. I must wisely choose who partakes in my life, and at what level. The deepest part of my heart is for Jesus only. When it comes to guys, I've found that I can have the blessing of friendship with other brothers in Christ and still keep my heart safely guarded by making sure that Christ is always my central focus. Feminine mystique isn't running from the opposite sex or hiding in the shadows—it is walking in the life and joy of Christ and allowing that to bless those around me through God-honoring interaction and life-giving friendship!

—BRIANNE, 29

the subject when a topic arises that doesn't bring glory to God. But if you don't send signals that indicate what your standard of purity is, how will a guy ever get the message that you are a set-apart young woman? How will he ever know that you expect something more from him as a Christ-professing man? How will he ever be inspired to rise to a higher standard?

When it comes to talking casually with guys, choose to exchange all foolish, idle, flirtatious conversation for edifying words that build faith and bring glory to God. Beware of downplaying spiritual things so that a guy doesn't think of you as strange. Let guys know without question where you stand—that Jesus Christ is the number one passion and focus of your life and heart. If a guy looks down on you for being consumed with Christ, he is not warrior-poet material anyway—and not worth your heart.

Many young women I've talked with feel restricted in talking about spiritual things with guys right off the bat. There seems to be a general feeling in modern Christianity that conversations about Christ and His Word should be reserved for deeper, more intimate friendships. But it's more than possible to engage in spiritual dialogue with guys you are just getting to know. In fact, that's *how* you build a friendship upon Jesus Christ.

One way I have learned to set myself apart for my future husband is by not striving to receive the approval or notice of men now. If I am interested in turning a man's head now, what will change once I get married? This is a challenge because we are taught to crave the attention of men and to gain our status from how many heads we can turn. I have seen how the Lord honors women who seek to honor Him and gain their confidence from Him alone.

—ASHLEY, 24

My friendship with Eric was hallmarked by spiritual conversation from the very first day I met him. Not only was he willing and eager to talk about Jesus

Christ, he didn't even seem to want to talk about anything else! Even though we didn't share intimate prayer times or personal stories about what God was doing at the deepest levels with our souls, our entire friendship was built upon mutual spiritual passion. We discussed Scripture, applied biblical truth in regard to cultural issues, shared stories of how we'd seen God work on mission trips and outreaches, and shared worship songs we'd written. There was an immediate like-mindedness between us, and cultivating spiritual discussion created more of a kindred bond and set the stage for a Christ-centered, Christ-focused, Christ-honoring friendship.

Don't shy away from steering your conversations with guys toward the things of God. It's one of the best ways to get to know a guy's true heart and build upon the right foundation from the very beginning. Of course, there are guys who might use spiritual things to try to manipulate your heart. Allow God's Spirit to give you discernment as you get to know a guy. If he asks you to share things that are too personal under the banner of "spiritual discussion," don't hesitate to let him know your boundaries. If you sense that he is merely saying all the right things but not truly living it out, it's a good idea to be cautious rather than charging ahead into the friendship. If you are led by the Spirit of God rather than your own emotions or impatience, your heart will be protected, and you will have wisdom and clarity in handling each and every situation you face.

And by the way, there are other ways to get to know a guy beyond just talking. Sharing experiences together goes a long way in acquainting you with someone's true heart. Participating in the same ministry ventures—such as inner-city outreaches or short-term missions trips—is a great way to share life experience without getting overly personal. Spending time together around your family members—as unexciting as that might sound—is an excellent way to see his true colors and let him see yours. Don't think that one-on-one discussion is the only way to build a friendship. Often, actions can speak about someone's character and heart far louder than words.

Show Decorum in Your Body Language

Not long ago, I stood in the midst of a large Christian gathering for young adults as people were congregating, socializing, and waiting for the meeting to begin. It was interesting to watch the physical interaction between the sexes. Guys teasingly tickling girls. Girls playfully tackling guys. Guys bellowing loud greetings and giving girls bear hugs. Girls giggling and jumping on guys' backs. The physical touch between men and women was aggressive and prevalent—not just among dating couples, but among casual friends and acquaintances. It's something Eric and I have seen in nearly every Christian group of singles and young adults we've visited. In a world where it's normal to have sex with a complete stranger, playful physical interaction among Christian guys and girls hardly seems worth making a fuss over. Compared to what the rest of the world is doing, it doesn't seem like a big deal. Why should we even make an issue out of it? After all, we don't want people to think we're stodgy and prudish, do we?

Interacting with guys, even Christian guys, usually involves a good amount of physical touch. Even if you barely know a guy, it's normal and accepted to hug him, hold his hand, stand close to him, put your arm around him, ruffle his hair, and playfully hit him. The casual, careless way that girls interact physically with guys is yet another indication of the decline of feminine dignity and mystique. It used to be the opposite. A girl wouldn't allow a man to touch her until he proved he was a gallant warrior-poet worthy of her heart. Even then, it was carefully measured and guarded—sacred things being saved for sacred moments. Women garnered respect from men because they didn't give their physical body—even in the form of casual touch—to any random guy they met. I remember hearing the story of my great-grandmother riding in the carriage with her groom-to-be on the way to their wedding. He leaned over to kiss her, and she pulled away, saying sweetly, "There will be plenty of time for that after the wedding!" These days, such a scene seems laughably ridiculous. But I think we could use a lot more of my great-grandmother's decorum in our modern femininity. Just take a quick peek at what God says about male/female interaction.

I will never forget when a group of my peers unofficially voted me "Last to Be Married." When I asked why, I was told that the kind of man I was looking for would be too hard to find. However, I am assured that God has a Christ-built man for me. I know I won't find him in worldly places but in service to his King. Yes, doubts and struggles still sometimes come, and it is not always easy to hold onto something that the world tells me is hopeless. Yet, God is faithful. His grace is all I need to walk in His truth. I continually pray that He will lead and guide me on this path I could not walk alone.

—Shauna, 21

> It is good for a man not to touch a woman (1 Corinthians 7:1).

Though some translations interpret this verse as "it is good for a man not to marry," in reality the word *touch* here means physical contact. It's the same word used all throughout the New

Testament for every kind of touch—even casual touch. Physical touch between men and women is very powerful and is not to be treated flippantly. Our Christian culture may make light of casual touch between guys and girls, but it's not a light thing to God. Our Maker designed physical touch between men and women to be the catalyst for sexual intimacy, and when that fire is ignited out of context, it leads to harm. As it says in Proverbs:

> Can a man take fire in his bosom, and his clothes not be burned? Can one go upon hot coals, and his feet not be burned? (Proverbs 6:27-28 KJV).

When you set your physical body "off limits" to the opposite sex, you guard the feminine intrigue and mystique that God created within you. It may seem that all guys enjoy girls who carelessly offer their bodies to be casually touched, but Christ-built guys are *fascinated, intrigued, and captivated* by women who are mysterious and guarded. Warrior-poets have far more respect for a woman who is guarded and discreet than one who is aggressive and cavalier with her body. As we discussed earlier, women have an incredible power to seduce. Even if it is not your intention to arouse lustful thoughts in the opposite sex, if you are flippant about your physical interaction with guys, you risk leading them to stumble sexually. You also send a compromising message about the sacredness (or lack thereof) of your body. It may be completely normal for every other Christian girl you know to be physical when interacting with guys. Casual touch and sensual behavior may be treated lightly among modern Christians. But what is God's perspective?

> Reproofs of instruction are the way of life, to keep you from the evil woman, from the flattering tongue of a seductress.

Do not lust after her beauty in your heart, nor let her allure you with her eyelids. For by means of a harlot a man is reduced to a crust of bread; and an adulteress will prey upon his precious life (Proverbs 6:23-26).

We must answer to God for the way we choose to use our feminine power. If we interact with guys in a sensual, flirtatious way, if we use our eyes, words, and body language to tempt him sexually, and if we are haphazard about physical touch, we are participating in the "way of the evil woman." God's prescription for male/female interaction is simple and straightforward:

Treat...younger women as sisters, with all purity (1 Timothy 5:2 NIV).

Purity in this verse is not just talking about maintaining physical virginity until marriage. It means "without sin." In other words, we need to be Christ-like and above reproach in *every dimension* of our interaction with the opposite sex and watchful and vigilant over our heart *and* the hearts of the guys in our lives.

When it comes to your body language toward guys, don't take your cues from pop culture, movies, or even your Christian friends. Instead, keep the sacredness of your relationship with your husband always in the forefront of your mind. You may not know his name, but every decision you make right now—big or small—in relating to the opposite sex will affect the purity and beauty of your future marriage.

So what kind of physical interaction *is* appropriate with a guy? Here's a great test question to ask in every situation: If you were married and your husband was standing next to you, would he feel comfortable with your actions? Eric wouldn't mind if I held another guy's hand during a group prayer, but he certainly wouldn't feel comfortable with me tickling another guy, standing super close to another guy, giving a tight hug to another guy, or jumping on another guy's back. Anything that you wouldn't do with another guy *after* marriage is something that you shouldn't do with another guy *before* marriage.

It doesn't matter if you think that you might one day marry the guy that you are getting to know. Until God makes it clear that this is your life-long covenant marriage partner, live as if you (and he) both belong to someone else. And even after you are in a relationship headed toward marriage, it is always healthy to be extra cautious and guarded in the area of physical touch (something we will talk about more, later in this book.) When in doubt, it's always best to err on the side of caution. Even if your standards seem old-fashioned, prudish, or extreme to others, why should that bother you? The only thing that matters is protecting the glory of your King and the sacredness of your future marriage. A warrior-poet will appreciate, respect, and cherish a woman who guards mystique and saves every aspect of her physical body as a sacred gift for him.

What should I do when I'm attracted to a guy?

Being attracted to a guy isn't wrong in itself. It's what you *do* with the attraction that defines whether you are honoring Christ or not. If you allow attraction toward a guy to overtake your thoughts and emotions, it can easily become an "idol" and take your focus off Christ. Attraction can quickly morph into an unhealthy emotional obsession with someone—clouding your relationship with your King and dishonoring your relationship with your future husband. If your actions and decisions are directed by attraction rather than the Spirit of God or if your mind is consumed with a guy rather than Jesus Christ, you know it's taken an unhealthy hold over you. But if you handle attraction right from the beginning, it doesn't need to become a stumbling block to remaining pure and set apart for Christ. Here are some practical suggestions for dealing with feelings of attraction.

I know of very few men whom I feel safe around spiritually and emotionally. I have noticed it would take a lot for most modern men to stand for anything.

Many modern men seem to think that they need to suppress the "warrior spirit" inside of them. I have only met a handful of men that truly seek to a live the life modeled after Christ—men who have a love of truth and a willingness to defend it.

—SHAUNA, 21

Give It to God

The best thing you can do when you feel attracted to a guy is to immediately give your feelings to God: *Lord, thank You for the qualities I see in this guy. Please take my emotions and guard them. Enable me to keep my heart protected for my future husband. If it is Your desire that I enter a relationship with this guy, then I leave the details in Your hands. May I not manipulate or grow impatient, but allow You to remain in complete control. You will be faithful. You care more about this area of my life than even I do.*

The guy you are attracted to might seem like the only warrior-poet in existence, and you might not be able to imagine living life without him. But the reality is that if he is not the one God wants you to marry, then the guy He *has* chosen for you will fit your life even more perfectly, and what you esteem in him will be even *more* than what you see in this guy. Don't allow your emotions to lead the way—take a step back and surrender them afresh to your loving Father. When your heart is fully yielded to Christ, you will be far more able to discern between His voice and the voice of your own desires.

Guard Your Thought Life

Many young women struggle with keeping their thoughts upon Christ—especially when there is a guy in their life to whom they are attracted. When you see an attractive and Christ-like guy, it's tempting to let your mind continually dwell on him and get carried away with imaginations, desires, and fantasies about him. Even a Christ-built warrior-poet can claim an unhealthy hold on your thought life if you are not guarded and purposeful about "taking every thought captive." It's not wrong to notice or think about a guy's good qualities, but to continually dwell on him day and night is not God's best for your mind, heart, or emotions. Ask God to enable you to keep your thoughts on Jesus Christ—not on a guy. If you continually struggle with an onslaught of distracting thoughts about a guy, you can take some proactive steps to shift the pattern. First, the moment the thoughts come in, immediately start praying. Yes, you can briefly pray for the guy you are thinking about, but it's better to pray for someone else so your prayers don't become another catalyst for obsessive thoughts. Pick someone in your life who needs the love of Christ and aggressively pray for that person's soul. Whenever the enemy tries to distract you, hit back by praying intensely for an unsaved person. It's one of the best strategies against spiritual attack. The enemy will back off when he realizes that it only turns you into a prayer warrior for the kingdom of God.

Memorizing and meditating upon Scripture is another excellent way to center your thoughts on Jesus Christ. Remember,

Christ is the "Word of God made flesh" so when you dwell on Scripture, you are dwelling on Him. At first it might feel mechanical to memorize verses and recite them in your mind to ward off distracting thoughts about a guy. However, you will find that after you get into the habit of doing it, it becomes life-giving and refreshing. When truth is in the forefront of your mind, you are far less likely to allow your emotions to carry you away and into a path of error.

Don't Act Differently Around Him

When you are attracted to a guy, it's easy to allow your emotions to change the way you act around him. Whether you go out of your way to be around him, ignore other people to talk to him, or change your behavior to get him to notice you, attraction can quickly morph into manipulation. Rather than trusting God to open up a relationship if and when He desires, you might feel an urgent need to take the situation in your own hands and make something happen. A great promise to remember during times like this is Psalm 37:4 (NASB), "Delight yourself in the LORD, and He will give you the desires of your heart." Your faithful King knows every longing, dream, and desire within your heart. If you leave the pen in His hands, He will be more than faithful to script the story in His own perfect way—not only meeting the desires of your heart, but going exceedingly and abundantly beyond all you could ask or think. Taking matters into your own hands will only diminish the beautiful work of God in your life. Ask Him for the grace to remain trusting and yielded—no matter how strong your feelings toward a guy might be. Let the Spirit of God guide your actions and convict you of any change in behavior that you've allowed because of your own impatience or fear that you might "miss your chance." He will be more than faithful if you simply give Him the chance to be who He says He is. As Psalm 34 declares:

> Oh, taste and see that the LORD is good; blessed is the man who trusts in Him! Oh, fear the LORD, you His saints; there is no want to those who fear Him. The young lions lack and suffer hunger; but those who seek the LORD shall not lack any good thing (Psalm 34:8-10).

These are not just poetic words, they are the very words of God to you, His precious daughter. Ask Him for the grace to trust Him with all your heart, especially in this area of your life, and you will not be disappointed. He is faithful!

How do I respond to a guy who shows interest in me?

Obviously, the answer to this question depends greatly upon the situation. Even if the guy who shows interest in you is someone you are excited about, be sure to seek God's heart before jumping in with both feet. When Eric and I began to think God might be moving us beyond a friendship into a serious relationship, the first thing we did was take a week apart to fast, pray, and seek God's heart. Though we were both drawn to each other and had seen God do amazing things in our friendship, we didn't want to hastily jump into a relationship until we were sure it was what our King desired for us. I am so thankful we took the time to be sure of God's will before we moved ahead. During that week of prayer, I felt God clearly speak to my heart about my future with Eric, not only through the time I spent seeking Him, but also through the wisdom and counsel of my godly teammates—my parents. I didn't want to give my heart—even in small ways—to someone who was not my future husband. Taking a step back to ask for God's wisdom gave me the confidence to move forward without uncertainty or fear. If a guy you are drawn to shows interest in you, the best thing you can do before moving forward is take a season to pray and seek God. Remember, even Christ-built warrior-poets must prove they are worthy of your heart. Don't offer yourself to a guy too readily. Rather, let him know that Jesus Christ is your first love and that, unless *He* is the one putting the relationship together, you have no interest in moving forward. As it says in the Psalms, "Unless the LORD builds the house, they labor in vain who build it" (Psalm 127:1).

It is also a great idea to go to your teammates, those who are outside the situation, and get godly counsel, prayer, and perspective. My parents actually knew before I did that Eric was the "one" because they had been praying for my future husband since I was two years old. Going to them and gaining their perspective was invaluable. They were able to provide both encouragement to move forward

I finally surrendered to the Lord the desire of my heart to get married. Making Him my first and foremost priority has helped me shape how I live set-apart for my husband. No longer am I searching for a husband so that he can fulfill all my needs, but I have come to understand that Christ must be the one to do that. By doing this I stopped seeking out attention from guys, stopped trying to date or find a husband, started guarding my heart for my future husband, and started understanding the incredible love relationship that God wants to have with me. I have begun to see that clinging to my desire to get married was hindering me from having a closer relationship with the One who gave everything to save me!

—NAOMI, 23

and caution where caution was needed. As I've said before, I never would have thought that having my parents involved in a relationship would have been romantic, but in reality I felt so loved, protected, and secure having them there—it honestly felt like a fairy tale. Even if you don't have parents who are in touch with the heart of God, going to the teammates He's placed in your life is such an important factor in gaining clarity and wisdom for relationship decisions.

Once you've established a clear understanding of romantic intentions in a relationship with a guy, it's still important to be guarded and God-directed. Eric and I have seen far too many couples start out with Christ at the center of their relationship and then take things into their own hands. Just because God is writing our love story doesn't mean that we can't take the pen out of His hands and derail it with our own agenda. We'll talk more about the practical side of this in the next chapter. Remember to keep your relationship with Christ far above your relationship with an earthly prince, and allow *Him* to be the One who truly meets and fulfills the desires of your heart.

So what if a guy you are *not* attracted to shows interest? Many young women try to make this situation a complicated process. But it doesn't need to be. Honest, clear, concise communication is always the best way to go. Simply telling the guy, nicely but clearly, that you are not interested is the first step. If you don't know him or have a friendship with him, there's no need to say anything more. Don't feel that you need to soften your words and leave yourself open to the possibility of something happening down the road. Don't think that in order to be polite you need to give him your phone number, email address, or access to your life. Most modern guys are trained to be aggressive toward girls, thinking that if they are persistent enough, they can whittle down a woman's resistance. That's why it is important to firmly close the door in the very beginning. If a guy won't take no for an answer, consider recruiting the help of a protector such as a dad, older brother, or godly leader in your life. Remember, guarding your heart, mind, and emotions for your future husband is more important than protecting the feelings of a guy you don't even know. If you can say no to the guy without hurting his feelings, then by all means do. But if you have to step on his toes a little to get your point across, don't hesitate to stand strong.

If you *do* have a friendship with the guy who shows interest in you, obviously there is more to be said than simply "No thanks, not interested." However, the same rule applies here. Don't soften your response by leaving the door open for the possibility of a relationship. It's far more considerate to close the door firmly than leave him constantly wondering if you might eventually change your mind. He needs the freedom to move past seeing you as a potential partner. It's fine to tell him that you appreciate his friendship and would like to continue being friends with him. But if you ever sense that he is trying to blur boundary lines or manipulate your heart under the banner of friendship, that's a sign that you need to back away from him as a friend. Keep your future husband's feelings in the forefront of your mind. If your future husband could see your friendship with this guy, would he feel completely honored and respected—not just by you, but also by the guy? If the answer to that question is ever "no," then it's clear this friendship does not belong in your life. No matter how awkward or even painful it might be to sever ties with an inappropriate guy friend, you will be blessed going to such lengths to preserve your heart and honor your future husband.

I am well aware that there are countless factors that play into every guy relationship you face in your life. There might be sticky or confusing situations that I cannot address in this book. That's why it is critical to keep your intimate, daily relationship with Jesus Christ at the center of your existence. Don't downplay the importance of spending ample time in prayer, in His Word, in seeking His voice and the direction of His Spirit. He *will* direct your steps if you are truly building your life around Him. And if you find yourself struggling to hear His voice or know His heart, consider taking a season to spend time in focused prayer and drawing near to Him. Even if you have to cut relationships, friendships, and activities out of your life, there is nothing more important than your personal walk with the Prince of Peace and Lover of your soul. And if you draw near to Him, He *will* draw near to you (see James 4:8). When He is in His rightful place, everything confusing in your life finally begins to make sense. Remember, He cares more about this area of your life than even you do! A life built around Jesus Christ is the best solution for any guy question you could ever face.

CHAPTER SEVEN

Fairy-Tale Love Stories

the blueprint for a Christ-built relationship

In a modern world ravaged by mindless sex and mediocre marriages, achieving a fairy-tale love story is no small accomplishment. The enemy of our souls seems to be extra aggressive these days in his attempts to ruin beautiful romances before they even begin. It makes sense, if you think about it. When relationships are built upon God's perfect pattern, they lead to strong, healthy, Christ-centered marriages. Strong, Christ-centered marriages lead to strong, Christ-centered families. And strong, Christ-centered families breed strong, Christ-centered churches and communities. Strong, Christ-centered churches and communities progress the kingdom of God and wage war on the kingdom of darkness. So it's no wonder Satan wants to destroy the beauty of God-scripted romance.

Two days ago Eric and I sat down with a soon-to-be-married couple who had moved from a vibrant, Christ-centered,

God-scripted romance to an impure, mediocre, run-of-the-mill "Christian" relationship in a matter of weeks. Selfish desires had taken over, Jesus Christ had been pushed to the back burner, and it didn't take long for the fairy-tale magic to disappear. It's something we've seen time and time again in our work with the younger generation. When it comes to honoring God in romance, what starts out with the best of intentions often ends with the worst of consequences.

So how can you avoid becoming one of the dismal statistics? That's what this chapter is all about. Even though I frequently see the sad results of people taking the pen into their own hands, I also hear the beautiful testimonies of those who left it completely in God's hands and reaped the remarkable rewards. Building a relationship 100 percent right is more than possible—even in today's relationship-challenged world. And it's God's passionate desire that you, His set-apart princess, will be among those who experience His very best.

Building a romance God's way is not a formula. God works differently in different people. However, there are certain principles that *always* govern a Christ-centered relationship. If you truly build your life and love story around these principles, you can be certain you'll experience a beautiful romance and avoid the heartache so common in our modern times.

Principle One: Keep Christ at the Center

If you've read any of my books, you know that my message is all about making Christ the focus of your entire existence. This principle isn't just to be lived out in theory, but in practical, day-to-day life. I can honestly say that making Christ my first love was *the* reason that my love story with Eric worked. Through the years I've seen many young Christians attempt to build a God-honoring relationship without a vibrant walk with Christ backing it up. Every time it falls apart. Without an active, daily, living, breathing, passionate relationship with Christ, it's nothing more than human wisdom and human effort attempting to reach the heights of heavenly romance. Without the power of Christ's Spirit, it simply can't be done. When I think about the early days of my love story with Eric, I don't just remember the wonder of falling in love and the beauty of discovering Eric's heart. I vividly remember falling in love with Jesus Christ and basking in the beauty of a romance with Him—a romance that was enhanced, not diminished, by my love story with Eric.

When my relationship with Eric began, everyone expected us to start living out the typical boyfriend/girlfriend pattern—becoming completely preoccupied with each other, spending every waking moment of our spare time together, expressing our physical affection for each other, and focusing our thoughts and conversations on our passionate feelings for each other. But we knew that God wanted something different for us. He wanted to remain at the center of our relationship—not just in theory, but in reality. We realized that if we started focusing on our feelings for each other rather than our mutual passion for Christ, we would push Him to the outside of our romance. So we entrusted our emotions to God. We asked Him to guard our hearts and not unlock passion for each other until the proper time.

In the meantime, we agreed to keep our conversation, focus, and energy centered on Jesus Christ and not each other. To most people it seemed strange. Here we were—a young couple in a serious relationship with the intention of getting married someday—and we didn't even act like we were dating. We didn't hold hands. We didn't kiss. We didn't sit close together on the couch and whisper into each other's ear. We didn't have long, ardent phone conversations. We didn't talk about our feelings for each other. We didn't spend time cuddling or gazing into each other's eyes. We didn't say "I love you." People who hadn't been directly told that there was something between us often didn't even realize we were a couple.

Instead, we encouraged each other to pursue more of Christ. We read Christian biographies and talked about how they impacted our lives. We shared stories about how God was working in our lives and what He was teaching us. We prayed for each other. We prayed together for other people we knew. We shared Scripture. We supported each other in the individual ministry steps God challenged us to take. We joined our church community and family in doing outreaches. While Eric spent several months away at missionary school, we talked on the phone about once a week and wrote each other letters of spiritual encouragement. (This happened before the days of email and cell phones, if you can believe it!)

I am well aware that the way Eric and I built our relationship seems outdated, restrictive and unromantic to many. But I want to tell you unequivocally that it was like a dream come true. Just think about what makes a Jane Austen romance so appealing. It's the slow, delicate process of one heart opening to another. In old-fashioned love stories, you don't carelessly fling your mind, emotions, and body upon someone the moment they say they like you. In fairy tales, you don't go from zero to sixty in seconds. You savor each conversation, carefully weigh each word, and patiently wait months or years before you finally win the priceless treasure of the other person's heart. Modern romances are sadly lacking in the dignity, nobility, and honor that was prevalent in the days of knights and fair maidens. The only way to gain the dignity and nobility that our feminine hearts crave is to carefully protect the sacred things, no matter how strange or old-fashioned they might seem.

Instead of spending mindless hours on the phone with Eric every night, I waited with eager anticipation for his once-a-week call he would make from the pay phone outside his missionary school. Every word was savored. We didn't waste time talking about meaningless things. We cherished every moment and counted every conversation as significant. It was a thousand times more special and romantic because we only talked once a week. Instead of exchanging quick, shallow emails every day, we took the time to write long, thoughtful letters to each other. I still love to look through the box of letters that we wrote to each other during those years. It reminds me of a Jane Austen novel. I look at the carefully scripted, thoughtful words and remember the delicate way our hearts opened to each other. It was a thousand times more romantic and dignified than mindless emails or text messages.

This is not to say that you can't have the "Jane Austen magic" if you choose to use email or cell phones in your love story! The principle that makes the fairy-tale spirit come alive is keeping sacred things sacred. Rather than allowing your communication with the other person to be careless and haphazard, allow God's Spirit to make every conversation, letter, email, and phone call *purposeful, thoughtful,* and *Christ-centered.*

Because we were committed to keeping Jesus Christ at the center of our conversations, phone calls, and letters, we were able to build a strong spiritual foundation for our relationship. All too many love stories that start out with a spiritual focus speedily shift to an emotion-led whirlwind. Once you allow your emotions to lead the way, spiritual things quickly get squeezed into the background. But when you build your communication and interaction around the things of God, your hearts are knit together in Him. As you draw closer to Christ, you naturally draw closer to each other—in a healthy, beautiful, Christ-led process rather than a lightning-speed, human-led, emotional roller coaster ride. As you make decisions about how to build your romance, don't take your cues from the rest of the world. Just because other Christian relationships look a certain way doesn't mean yours should. As I said, when Eric and I built our relationship, it appeared strange, extreme, unnecessary and even legalistic to others. But as we followed the lead of God's Spirit and not the trends of culture, we found a taste of heaven on earth.

Don't be afraid of putting physical distance between you and your future husband. People often feel a pressure to be together on a continual basis during a blossoming romance, thinking that it might fall apart if they are not around each other 24/7. But if God wants your relationship to stay together, it will remain strong no matter how many miles, months, or years separate you from each other. I believe that being geographically separated from Eric during the majority of our love story was a huge factor in keeping our focus on Christ rather than each other and in keeping the magic and mystery alive throughout the entire process. Take some time to prayerfully consider putting distance between you and your significant other to cultivate a Spirit-led, Christ-focused love story. It's a great way to freshly surrender the relationship back to Christ and make sure that He is always honored above your human emotions and desires.

Often love stories that begin as God-scripted fairy tales can morph into human-led emotional flings. This happens whenever Jesus Christ is removed from His rightful position as the first and foremost love of your life. Be on guard against losing your own individual relationship with Christ as your love story unfolds. While it's certainly important to think and pray about your love story, don't allow all of your thoughts, journal entries, and prayers to center around the guy you are falling in love with. Rather, cultivate your individual intimacy with Christ—apart from the relationship that is forming. Meditate on His character, listen to His voice, study His Word, and make plenty of time for heartfelt worship. As young women, it's easy to transfer our affection for Christ onto our future husband—to lose our spiritual vitality as we become caught up in the drama and emotion of a human romance. But unless Jesus Christ remains our first love, we will always be looking to a mere human to meet the deepest needs in our heart, and we'll always be disappointed because they are needs that only Christ can meet.

My greatest challenge as a single young woman is learning contentment in whatever state I am in. It is extremely easy to grow discontent and take my attention and focus off of Christ, especially when I see the wonderful love stories of my friends unfolding. I depend on God's help daily to help me to be content with where He has me for today. I realize the importance of keeping my eyes on Him, allowing Him to shape and mold my life. As I focus on God, I find it far easier to trust Him—that if it is His will, in His perfect time, He will orchestrate a God-written love story that is beyond my imagination.

—JESSICA, 21

Your romance with Christ is not supposed to be a stand-in until you finally meet the man you'll marry. Your romance with Christ is meant to be the lifelong passion of your heart and soul. Your earthly love story should *pale* in comparison to your love story with Christ—not just during your single years, but every day for the rest of your life. And if it ever comes down to a choice between Christ and your future husband, Jesus Christ must *always* come first. In my book *Set-Apart Femininity*, I wrote about one of my heroes, Sabina Wurmbrand, who was willing to be separated from her husband and son for ten years and suffered unspeakable tortures and heartache to protect the name of Christ. Sabina loved her husband—but she loved Jesus Christ more. This is what it means, in practical terms, to make our King the first and foremost love of our heart. He tells us:

> If anyone comes to Me and does not hate his father and mother, wife and children, brothers and sisters, yes, and his own life also, he cannot be My disciple (Luke 14:26).

A God-scripted, earthly love story is a beautiful thing. But if it ever usurps Christ's position in your heart and life, it becomes an idol that must be removed. Nothing is worth sacrificing our relationship with the true Lover of our soul.

Even now, after many years of marriage to Eric, I must constantly remember that my husband is not to be the focal point of my existence—Jesus Christ is. Eric is not to be the one who brings the deepest fulfillment, comfort, security, and joy to my soul—Jesus Christ is. To keep our marriage alive and beautiful, both of us must vigilantly guard our individual romance with Christ. When He is at the center, everything else falls perfectly into place.

Principle Two: Vigilantly Protect Purity

A young engaged couple recently we know confessed to allowing sexual compromise into their relationship. They didn't technically have sex, but they did almost everything up to that point, all the while assuming that they were still protecting their purity. "I just didn't think it was really that big of a deal to God," the young woman told us. "I mean, we're planning to get married anyway. We've committed our lives to each other. What's wrong with expressing our love physically prior to saying the wedding vows?"

That young woman articulated a very common attitude among modern Christians. We might believe that having casual sex with random people isn't God's best, but most of us don't see the significance of vigilantly guarding premarriage purity once you have pledged your life and heart to someone. So how big a deal is purity to God, anyway? If you love someone and know you are going to get married, why is it so important to hold back?

The reason we don't understand the importance of purity is because we don't understand the significance of the marriage covenant. A wedding isn't merely a ceremony in which you verbally commit to love each other for the rest of your lives. A wedding is a sacred exchange—a holy covenant in which two lives become one. Until you have entered into that covenant, you are still individuals—no matter how committed you might be to the relationship. Once you enter that sacred covenant, you are no longer two individuals, but "one flesh." Then and only then are you free to enjoy each other's bodies in an intimate way, entering into the "holy of holies" without shame. (Note: In the Jewish Temples, the "holy of holies" was the most sacred, intimate place—the place where the very presence of God dwelled. Jews did not enter it lightly or flippantly. In a marriage relationship, the "holy of holies" can be likened to sexual intimacy—the most sacred, intimate form of communicating with another person—and must not be treated carelessly. For more detail about this principle, please read *Set-Apart Femininity*.)

If you engage in sensual touch prior to entering that sacred covenant, you dishonor God's perfect design and leave yourselves wide open for the enemy to ravage the beauty and nobility of your relationship. God's Word says:

> Marriage is to be held in honor among all, and the marriage bed is to be undefiled; for fornicators and adulterers God will judge (Hebrews 13:4 NASB).

When we choose to engage in sexual intimacy prior to a covenant exchange, we dishonor the sanctity and holiness of marriage. The word *fornication* in Scripture might seem vague at first glance, but there is nothing vague about it. According to God's pattern, *any sexual expression* outside of the marriage covenant is considered fornication. To keep sex sacred, we must keep *all* expressions of sexual intimacy sacred. Sexual touch of any kind is an intimate "knowing" of another person—and such intimate acts, in God's pattern, are only meant as an outflow of a holy marriage covenant. When we read the Song of Solomon, we discover that it is not just the act of sex, but all forms of intimate touch and expression that are reserved for the "holy of holies" alone. (Interesting side note: You will not find oral sex mentioned among the beautiful expressions of physical intimacy in God's perfect pattern as outlined in the Song of Solomon. So if you are wondering whether oral sex even after marriage is appropriate, let that be your guide. We can never improve upon the way God designed a man and woman to express their love—our own methods will only warp and degrade it.)

This may sound strange, but Eric and I decided not to even kiss until our wedding day. We wanted to go out of our way to keep every form of intimacy sacred. My dad had once told us, "Anything physical that you save for marriage will only be more beautiful and fulfilling as time goes on. Anything that you experience beforehand will eventually lose its luster." When we put this wisdom into practice, we found it to be true. Even to this very day, whenever we share a kiss, it is just as beautiful, thrilling, and satisfying as it was on our wedding day. Instead of asking the question "how far is too far?" God challenged us to start asking a new question—"how far can we possibly go to honor Him in this area of our lives?" And as we made it our goal to live without even a hint of impurity in our physical relationship, we discovered that God's ways are truly beautiful and perfect. Because we saved everything in our physical relationship, it has only grown more and more amazing, fulfilling, and exciting with each year of our marriage.

I used to feel the need to qualify or downplay the fact that Eric and I didn't kiss until our wedding day. It seemed so extreme and unnecessary to people, and I didn't want them to think that I was judging them if they chose to kiss before marriage. So I went out of my way to say apologetically, "Eric and I chose not to kiss until our wedding day, but that doesn't mean *you* need to do that—it's really not a big deal either way."

But in recent years, my attitude has changed. While I certainly don't believe it's a sin to kiss prior to marriage, I've seen too many purity-esteeming couples compromise along the way because they didn't want to be too extreme about their standards. And every time they end up with a human-led, mediocre romance rather than the stunningly beautiful, heaven-on-earth fairy-tale version of love God intends. But when couples vigilantly *protect* the physical purity of their relationship at all costs, even going to what seems to be extremes to save *everything* for the sacred covenant exchange of marriage, God honors and blesses the relationship with more beauty and heavenly romance than they could have ever hoped for or dreamed of. Even something as innocent as kissing before marriage can subtly erode the sheen of purity in a love story—especially certain *kinds* of kissing! It's not that God can't still bless a marriage when physical things have been allowed into a relationship prior to marriage. But it could have been *even better*. It could have been an unclouded picture of heaven on earth—a vision of the most stunning, spectacular, brilliant purity this world has ever seen.

The more physical expression you allow into a relationship prior to marriage, the more you allow emotions and selfish desires rather than the Spirit of God to lead the way. Physical touch is a powerful and dangerous thing, and that's why it's meant to be saved for the "holy of holies" alone. If you want a relationship that is truly directed by God rather than your own selfish whims and agendas, then go to all lengths to vigilantly guard the physical purity of your relationship. Most modern Christians are so concerned about being extreme that they justify treating purity lightly. But I believe we should be far more concerned about violating God's standard for righteousness than coming across as extreme in our standards.

Once a violation of purity has been allowed into a relationship (even if you haven't *technically* had sex), your ability to hear God's voice becomes clouded. You think you are hearing the Spirit of God when in reality you are only hearing the voice of your own selfish desires. Purity is not something to mess with or take lightly.

Jesus Christ cannot remain at the center of a romance in which your own agenda is leading the way. Scripture is very clear on how seriously we are to take the protection of purity in our lives.

> Do not be deceived. Neither fornicators, nor idolaters, nor adulterers, nor homosexuals, nor sodomites, nor thieves, nor covetous, nor drunkards, nor revilers, nor extortioners will inherit the kingdom of God. Now the body is not for sexual immorality but for the Lord, and the Lord for the body. Do you not know that your bodies are members of Christ? Flee sexual immorality. Every sin that a man does is outside the body, but he who commits sexual immorality sins against his own body. Or do you not know that your body is the temple of the Holy Spirit who is in you, whom you have from God, and you are not your own? For you were bought at a price; therefore glorify God in your body and in your spirit, which are God's (1 Corinthians 6:9-10,13,15,18-20).

When God talks about fleeing sexual immorality, He doesn't mean to be cavalier about all physical expression up until the point of technically having sex. He means to *run away* from *anything* that would compromise the purity of the sacred marriage covenant He designed between a man and a woman.

> But fornication and all uncleanness or covetousness, let it not even be named among you, as is fitting for saints (Ephesians 5:3).

The phrase "not even be named among you" literally means that there is *not to be even a hint* of uncleanness or sexual impurity in our lives. When God prescribes that young men and women treat each other as brothers and sisters in all purity, He means it (see 1 Timothy 5:2). Even if you are in a serious relationship with someone, that doesn't give you a justifiable reason to engage in sensual touch prior to your wedding day. Until you enter into a sacred marriage covenant, you are to treat him as a brother in all purity. Think about what that means. Would you kiss your younger brother on the mouth? Would you wrap your arms around him sensually? Would you rest your hand on his thigh or allow him to rest his hand on yours? Would you sidle up to him on the coach and whisper "sweet nothings" into his ear? (If you would, then it's probably time to address some serious issues with your sibling relationships!) It may sound extreme to treat your serious boyfriend or fiancé the same way you would your brother, but that is God's prescription. In fact, He goes as far as to say that if there is any temptation toward compromise in a premarriage relationship, the couple should go ahead and get married in order to avoid sexual sin.

> But if they cannot exercise self-control, let them marry. For it is better to marry than to burn with passion (1 Corinthians 7:9).

When it comes to protecting the purity of your premarriage relationship, there is no such thing as being too extreme. And we must be specific rather than vague about our commitments in the area of physical purity prior to marriage. Here are a few practical pointers that can help make this happen.

- At the very beginning of the relationship, sit down and have a clear-cut conversation about your physical boundaries. Don't make decisions based on other people's standards. Look to the standard of Christ alone. Remember, instead of coming from the vantage point of "how far is too far?" we should be asking, "how far can we possibly go to honor our King in this relationship?" If the guy you're in a relationship with is putting pressure on you (even in subtle ways) to lower your physical standards, that's a clear sign that it's time to take a step back from the relationship and allow God to shape him into a selfless protector rather than a selfish conqueror of purity. A true warrior-poet will value and honor your desires for purity far above his own agenda. He will not make you feel guilty or strange for having high standards. He will esteem and respect you all the more for keeping vigilant watch over the treasure of your purity. If you are with a guy who does anything less, he is not yet truly worthy of your heart. And by the way, if either you or he is worried about purity leading to frigidity or sexual incompatibility in marriage, I can tell you with absolute confidence that this concern has no validity whatsoever. When you follow God's pattern, you experience the *fullness* of what He intended sexuality to be in marriage. Saving kissing and physical touch for your wedding day does *not* lead to sexual challenges in marriage. Rather, it leads to the most pure, beautiful, unhindered form of physical intimacy you could ever hope for or dream of.

• Share your specific commitments with accountability partners, such as your parents or godly teammates, and invite them to frequently ask bold questions about how you are doing in protecting the purity of the relationship. It's helpful for each of you to have your own separate accountability partners whom you can get together with on a regular basis. Give them permission to ask specific questions, such as "what kind of physical touch are you allowing into the relationship?" or "are you maintaining the commitments you've made before God?" It might seem awkward or uncomfortable at first, but knowing that you have to answer to someone every week about the physical aspect of your relationship is a wonderful way to guard against subtle compromise. In reality, this is one of the best and most practical ways that your teammates can serve your relationship—by working with you to carefully protect the things that are most sacred to your King.

• Set boundaries around "alone time." Don't just assume that because you've set specific physical boundaries in your relationship it's safe to spend hours alone together without temptation. Late nights sitting in the car, long hikes alone in the woods, nestling in the back of a dark movie theater, long talks alone in an empty house—all such scenarios give sexual compromise an unfair advantage. It doesn't matter how strong you feel in handling temptation, there is never a good reason to purposefully place yourself in a situation that can lead to compromise. God's Word makes it clear that sexual stumbling comes upon even the strongest of men, ending with disastrous results.

> With her enticing speech she caused him to yield, with her flattering lips she seduced him. Immediately he went after her, as an ox goes to the slaughter, or as a fool to the correction of the stocks, till an arrow struck his liver. As a bird hastens to the snare, he did not know it would cost his life. Now therefore, listen to me, my children; pay attention to the words of my mouth: Do not let your heart turn aside to her ways, Do not stray into her paths; for she has cast down many wounded, and all who were slain by her were strong men. Her house is the way to hell, descending to the chambers of death (Proverbs 7:21-27).

Giving sway to impurity seems so right in the heat of the moment. Sexual temptation is very much like the above-mentioned harlot in Proverbs. It entices us with sweet-sounding reasons about how harmless and beautiful it is to physically express our love. But with each step down the path of impurity, we venture further away from the perfect design and sacred intent of our King. And soon we end up with only a shell of a God-written love story—a relationship that proclaims to honor Christ but in reality only honors self. That's a shaky and dangerous foundation upon which to build a marriage.

When Eric and I were first married, a Christian leader took notice of the fact that we had "wisdom beyond our years" about spiritual things. He felt that the reason we had been blessed with unusual spiritual insight was because we'd protected the purity of our relationship prior to marriage. We'd listened to God's Spirit above our own fleshly desires, and as a result, we had cultivated the ability to hear His voice without the cloudiness and confusion that compromise so often brings. Honoring and protecting purity did so much more than merely enhance the romance in our marriage relationship. It strengthened our relationship with Jesus Christ and encouraged us to build our marriage upon the foundation of His amazing strength.

So I no longer apologize for the fact that Eric and I didn't kiss until our wedding day. I no longer act sheepish when I talk about the Jane Austen dignity that marked our love story. Esteeming purity in all its glory—and going to every extreme necessary to guard it—is what made our God-written love story a taste of heaven on earth. And I hope with all of my heart that you will experience the depths of Christ-centered romance the way that we did.

Principle Three: Experience God's Restoration

When I describe the level of purity and innocence that marked my relationship with Eric, it may seem hard to believe that we both came from very *impure* backgrounds. Eric and I grew up in Christian homes and went to youth group, but like most Christian young people today, we approached purity from a selfish vantage point. We constantly asked, "how far is too far?" rather than "how far can I possibly go to please God and honor my future spouse?" As a result, our lives were full of sin, selfishness, and compromise. Both of us gave our hearts, minds, emotions and bodies carelessly away in temporary flings, even though we technically kept our virginity. For most of our young adult lives, saving a kiss until our wedding day would have been the last thing either of us would have considered doing.

By the time I caught a vision for the amazing purity and breathtaking beauty that marked a Christ-centered love story, I honestly felt like it was too late for me to ever experience it. Sure, I'd technically kept my abstinence commitment, but my purity had been forsaken long ago. I'd allowed the treasure of my heart, emotions, and body to be trampled time and time again. I knew I was unworthy of a God-written love story.

But then, in His gentle, tender, patient way, my King began to show me that I could be completely washed clean, restored, and made new. If I was willing to repent and receive His forgiveness, I could be set free from all the baggage of the past, cleansed from all the impurity I'd allowed into my life. And I could experience the fullness of a brilliantly pure, God-scripted love story through the power of His redemption. It seemed almost too good to be true, but it was exactly what He promised.

God-scripted love stories are not just for those who have never compromised. In fact, the very reason that Christ sacrificed everything for us was to offer us the chance to be restored, washed clean, and given a hope and future. Just look at this amazing picture of Christ's heart toward those of us who have sinned.

> And when the scribes and Pharisees saw Him eating with the tax collectors and sinners, they said to His disciples, "How is it that He eats and drinks with tax collectors and sinners?" When Jesus heard it, He said to them, "Those who are well have no need of a physician, but those who are sick. I did not come to call the righteous, but sinners, to repentance" (Matthew 2:16-17).

If you feel that you've "gone too far" to experience a truly pure and beautiful God-scripted love story, let me assure you that it's *never* too late to be restored and made new by His amazing cleansing blood.

Repentance means turning and walking the other direction. Once you awaken to the fact that you are heading over a cliff, simply stop, turn, ask God's forgiveness, and then, by His grace, head in the other direction. There is no reason to look back or second-guess your position as His child. You should not expect a second-rate version of romance. Once you have been restored by Him, you are clothed in His righteousness. You are entitled to all the benefits of His amazing kingdom. Your forgiveness is complete. Your sin is removed as far from you as the east is from the west. It is finished.

We only need to read God's Word to know for certain that He did pay the price for our sins, once and for all. We should never cheapen His amazing sacrifice by wondering whether His work on the cross was truly sufficient. And we shouldn't try to improve ourselves before coming to Him in repentance. We shouldn't focus on our unworthiness. Instead, focus on His conquering, redeeming, transforming power, His precious blood shed on our behalf. Once you've been forgiven and set free, you are ready and able to experience His very best in the area of romance.

If you are *currently* in a relationship and have allowed impurity or compromise to enter in, there are some practical steps you might need to take to reestablish Christ as the center of this area of your life. Here are some practical suggestions for starting fresh and being made new.

Take a Step Back from the Relationship

As hard as it might seem, it's wise to take a season away from the relationship to let Christ fully remake and retrain you. Remember how Christ says we are to deal with sin?

> If your right eye causes you to sin, pluck it out and cast it from you; for it is more profitable for you that one of your members perish, than for your whole body to be cast into hell. And if your right hand causes you to sin, cut it off and cast it from you; for it is more profitable for you that one of

your members perish, than for your whole body to be cast into hell (Matthew 5:29-30).

Our King tells us that once we awaken to the fact that we've allowed sin into our lives, we are not to continue doing the things that led to our stumbling. That means if you were an alcoholic, you should no longer hang out in bars, sipping beer. If you were addicted to Internet porn, you should no longer spend hours alone, surfing the Internet. And if you stumbled sexually, you shouldn't remain in intense, close contact with the one you stumbled with. You need to "cut off" the thing that caused you to sin—namely, the relationship you are in. This isn't to say that God can't heal, restore, and cleanse a relationship and rebuild it upon a foundation of purity. But there needs to be a recalibration—new patterns need to be established, Christ needs to claim the throne in your life once again, and purity needs to govern your every action and thought.

When you are in the heat of an intense, emotional relationship with someone, you aren't able to truly allow Christ to renew and retrain your habits. You become distracted by your feelings for the other person, and it's all too easy to fall right back into the same sin over and over again. Even though it might be difficult, honor Christ by taking a step back from the relationship, surrendering it afresh to Him, and letting Him rebuild it only after a long season of healing, renewal, retraining, and restoration has been established. By taking a step away from the relationship, I'm not talking about a few days or a couple of weeks. If it's only been a short time, emotions are is still too fresh and old habits are still too familiar. It's a breeding ground for more compromise. Be willing to honor Christ and place Him first by walking away from the relationship indefinitely. And if He wants to rebuild it after several months or years, then He can. But be sure you are truly being directed by

His Spirit and not your own impatience or selfish desires. (Note: A situation involving an illegitimate pregnancy usually warrants an exception to this principle. If the relationship you are in is healthy [not verbally or physically abusive, etc.] then the best course of action is likely marriage for the sake of your child. If you are in that situation, I would strongly suggest gaining biblical marriage counseling from a trusted pastor or Christian leader. God is more than capable of fully redeeming everything that was lost and giving you a fresh start, but you'll need support and prayer as you walk through this process.)

Recruit Accountability Partners

When you've allowed sexual sin into your life, it's important to bring godly teammates into the picture. As difficult as it might be, Christ says that we are to "confess our sins one to another" (James 5:16). This does not mean you need to tell people the specific details of your sexual sin. Rather, it's acknowledging that you've stumbled and allowing the body of Christ to surround you with love, prayer, and encouragement as you seek to make things right in your life. You need faithful partners who will keep you accountable to your commitment to letting Christ regain His position as the ruler of your existence. If you've taken a step away from a compromising relationship, it can be extremely tempting to go running back to it after only a few days or weeks. Let your godly teammates hold you accountable, making sure that you don't make rash decisions based upon emotion or impatience. And the next time God leads you into a romantic relationship, whether it's with the same person or someone new, you will need an extra measure of accountability to walk in purity and not allow compromise to slip back in.

Once we've allowed sexual sin into our lives, it's easy for us to slip back into old patterns. It's extra important to remain vigilant and watchful and to submit to the loving counsel and accountability of people who have God's heart for us. Opening yourself up to accountability partners might seem uncomfortable. But it's one of the most important ways that we can "go to all lengths" to keep our hearts and lives pure before God. When you care more about pleasing Him than serving your own selfish comforts and desires, that's when you truly experience His fullness.

Fairy-tale love stories are more than possible, even in today's perverse and warped generation. But don't expect to find a fairy tale by imitating the haphazard, hold-nothing-back version of romance you see all around you. Only when you are willing to become one of the few in this generation who will go to all lengths to serve and honor your King and hold God's perfect design in the highest esteem, will you experience His very best in this area of your life. As I've said repeatedly in this book, He cares more about this than even you do! Leave the pen in His capable hands, and you will never be disappointed with the spectacular story He scripts. And even if His plan and purpose for you is not marriage (some of my greatest heroes in Christian history never married), you can be assured that every romantic dream in your heart can be completely fulfilled in a beautiful, intimate, lifelong, and eternal romance with the Prince and Lover of your soul—Jesus Christ.

Final Thoughts

what makes a woman truly
beautiful to a Christ-built man?

Can warrior-poet masculinity reemerge in this generation? Absolutely! God is very interested in shaping men into valiant, mighty, heroic examples of His strength and love. You may not think that your contributions can make much of a dent in the overall scheme of things, but all throughout Scripture, God demonstrates that it only takes *one* willing and yielded soul to change a generation. Keep your eyes on Jesus—the ultimate warrior-poet—and He will do amazing things through your life.

What does a warrior-poet truly desire in a woman? It's not a pretty face, a perfect figure, or a charming personality that will captivate his heart. Rather, it's complete abandonment to Jesus Christ. Just look at these inspiring responses from some God-fearing young men when I asked them what they desired most in a woman.

Purity, loyalty, and joy. But not for me—for God. A woman who desires to keep her relationship pure, loyal, and joyful with her Prince of Peace will then keep her relationship toward me pure, loyal, and joyful. All things that she does for her King, she will, in essence, be doing for me as well. A living example of the love of God and a lily among thorns.

—RICH, 24

Love, reverence, and obsession with her Lord. Love, support, encouragement, and even accountability toward me when it's necessary. Spiritual purity and a love for Christ so big she might burst.

—JOSH, 21

Mystique. Looking at a woman and being mystified by the depths of her soul. Looking at the surface and seeing beauty, kindness, gentleness, peace and joy, but knowing it doesn't stop there. Knowing that the heart and soul of the woman is a never-ending well, full of these gifts that triumph in all circumstances because she is Christ's dwelling place.

—BOBBY, 24

A woman who is solely focused on Jesus. A woman who intimidates me by her depth in the Word. A woman who cares more about what Jesus thinks than what the world around her thinks. A woman who has such depth that I will have to spend all eternity diving into the mystery of who she is. A woman who is focused on me before we even meet (as in not giving away her heart or body to every guy that comes her way and feeling no need to flirt and attract attention—but rather, she is treasuring the mystery and majesty of who she is). A woman who is entirely self-less. A woman who does not point to and lift up herself but continually shifts people's focus to Jesus. A woman who would rather spend time with Jesus than with me.

—NATHAN, 23

A genuine, close relationship with God. This means she is constantly praying. It means that she doesn't depend on the world (or even me) for her happiness, but only her Father. It means that she is loving and merciful because she is spending so much time with Love Himself. It means she isn't living a fake form of Christianity, and it means that she has her eyes set on the right goal. And if her life is right with God, then all the other aspects of her life will be in good hands.

—TIM, 21

A woman who won't settle for anything less than Christ's best. No matter what pain or uncomfortable feeling comes, she is willing to bring up any issue if it brings God glory. A woman who can challenge a man to love his Savior more is one of the most amazing and attractive qualities a woman could ever have. A faithful woman of prayer is someone I would love to spend the rest of my life with because I know there would never be a boring moment. Jesus is not boring, nor are the things of His kingdom! To spend the rest of my life advancing the kingdom with my future wife would be the greatest adventure any man could ever embark upon.

—BRANDON, 26

A woman who loves God more than she loves me. A woman who relies on Him for her strength and not on me. Granted, I want her to love me greatly, and I desire to be the kind of man she can trust and rely on, but God must be her rock. A woman who is completely sold out, wanting nothing more and nothing less than God's will and Christ's power in her life is remarkably attractive. A man seeking after God truly cannot help but be attracted to a young woman who is also seeking God with every last ounce of her strength.

—JEREMY, 20

When Ruth won Boaz' heart, it was not her looks or personality that drew him. Rather, he said to her:

And now, my daughter, do not fear. I will do for you all that you request, for all the people of my town know that you are a virtuous woman (Ruth 3:11).

If you long to turn a man's heart and not just his head, remember God's pattern:

Charm is deceitful and beauty is passing, but a woman who fears the LORD, she shall be praised (Proverbs 31:30).

No matter how helpless you've felt toward masculinity in the past, the ability to restore fairy-tale beauty to this earth rests right at your fingertips. You and I may never possess the physical appeal of a Victoria's Secret model (such beauty is fake, fleeting, and empty anyway). But possessing the stunning beauty of Christ is possible for every young woman who will simply yield her life to Him. And *that's* the kind of beauty that will both ravish the heart of a heroic earthly prince and change the face of masculinity forever.

Notes

Introduction: A Christ-Consumed Heart

1. Reprinted by permission of the publisher: 1998, John Waller Publishing (ASCAP), Gray Porch Publishing (BMI).

Chapter One: Counterfeit Manhood

1. Nielsen/Net Ratings, September 2003, http://www.covenanteyes.com/help_and_support/article/internet_pornography (accessed September 17, 2008).

2. Family Safe Media, December 15, 2005, http://www.covenanteyes.com/help_and_support/article/internet_pornography (accessed September 17, 2008).

3. Family Safe Media, January 10, 2006, http://www.covenanteyes.com/help_and_support/article/internet_pornography (accessed September 17, 2008).

4. Christianity Today Leadership Survey, December 2001, http://www.covenanteyes.com/help_and_support/article/internet_pornography_danger_statistics (accessed September 17, 2008).

5. John Eldredge, *Wild at Heart* (Nashville, TN: Nelson Books, 2001), 193-94.

6. Joe Zwales, "Metro Sexual Man and Proud of It," http://www.articlecity.com/articles/men/article_66.shtml (accessed September 16, 2008).

7. Alexa Hackbarth, "Vanity, Thy Name Is Metrosexual," *The Washington Post*, November 17, 2003, http://www.wordspy.com/words/metrosexual.asp (accessed September 16, 2008).

8. http://www.urbandictionary.com/define.php?term=metro-sexual (accessed September 16, 2008).

9. Eric Ludy, *The Bravehearted Gospel* (Eugene, OR: Harvest House Publishers, 2008), 59.

10. Wendy Shalit, *Girls Gone Mild* (New York: Random House, Inc, 2007), 5.

Chapter Two: Warrior-Poet Manhood

1. Eric Ludy, *God's Gift to Women* (Sisters, OR: Multnomah Publishers, 2003), 62.

2. Leslie Ludy, *Authentic Beauty* (Sisters, OR: Multnomah Publishers, 2003), 159.

Chapter Three: Unlocking Your Feminine Power

1. Karen Lee-Thorp, *Waking Up from a Dream of a Lifetime* (Colorado Springs, CO: Navpress, 2005), back cover.

Chapter Four: Heroic Womanhood

1. Leslie Ludy, *Set-Apart Femininity* (Eugene, OR: Harvest House Publishers, 2008), 28.

Chapter Five: Becoming a Princess of Purity

1. Published with the permission of Christa Taylor.

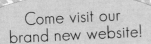
Come visit our brand new website!

www.SETAPART*girl*.com

Daily encouragement for your set-apart journey!

A message from Leslie:

Living as a set-apart young women in today's world is not easy. I invite you to visit setapartgirl.com for encouragement, inspiration, and fellowship with other like-minded young women.

Setapartgirl.com is my way of connecting with you, cheering you on, and providing you with the tools you need to live this message out on a day-to-day, moment-by-moment basis. You'll find blogs, articles, interviews, podcasts, event info, a discussion forum and lots of peeks into my life, family, and daily walk with Christ.

Hope to see you there!

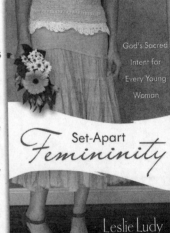